WOULDA/COULDA/SHOULDA

Other Books by Dr. Arthur Freeman

The Practice of Cognitive Therapy
Cognitive Therapy of Personality Disorders (with A. T. Beck)
Clinical Applications of Cognitive Therapy (with J. Pretzer,
    B. Fleming, and K. M. Simon)
Cognitive Therapy with the Suicidal Patient (with M. Rei-
    necke)
Depression and the Family (edited with N. Epstein and
    K. M. Simon)
Comprehensive Handbook of Cognitive Therapy (edited with
    K. M. Simon, L. Butler, and H. Arkowitz)
Cognition and Psychotherapy (edited with M. J. Mahoney)
Cognitive Therapy: Applications in Medical and Psychiatric
    Settings (edited with V. Greenwood)
Cognitive Therapy with Couples and Groups (edited)

Other Books by Rose DeWolf

The Bonds of Acrimony
The Best Defense (with Joel Moldovsky)
How to Raise Your Man (humor)

WOULDA / COULDA / SHOULDA

OVERCOMING REGRETS, MISTAKES, AND MISSED OPPORTUNITIES

Arthur Freeman, Ph.D.
AND
Rose DeWolf

PREFACE BY AARON T. BECK, M.D.

Silver Arrow Books
William Morrow
NEW YORK

Library of Congress Cataloging-in-Publication Data

Freeman, Arthur M.
    Woulda/coulda/shoulda: overcoming regrets, mistakes, and missed
opportunities/Arthur Freeman and Rose DeWolf.
        p.   cm.—(Silver arrow books)
    Includes index.
    ISBN 0-688-08508-3
    1. Cognitive therapy—Popular works.   2. Self-care, Health.
    I. DeWolf, Rose.   II. Title.
    RC489.C63F74   1989
    616.89'142—dc20   89-31854
                                                                         CIP

Printed in the United States of America

        4 5 6 7 8 9 10

BOOK DESIGN BY BRIAN MOLLOY

For Sloane and John
Who are not stuck in the past
and
For Karen and Bernie
With whom we look forward to the future

PREFACE

by Aaron T. Beck, M.D.
Director of the Center for Cognitive Therapy
and
University Professor of Psychiatry at the University of
Pennsylvania

In the thirty years since I first developed the therapeutic approach that has come to be called cognitive therapy, I have derived great satisfaction from seeing a number of my students, later colleagues, build upon my original work in depression and anxiety to resolve a wide range of psychological difficulties.

Arthur Freeman is one of these. In the dozen years that Art has been with me at the Center for Cognitive Therapy at the University of Pennsylvania, he has become one of the major teachers of cognitive therapy in the world today. His professional publications on the application of cognitive therapy and his recent collaborative work in the area of personality disorders has brought him recognition within the therapeutic community.

I was immensely pleased, then, when Art told me he was collaborating with Rose DeWolf in the writing of this book. A sensitive journalist, Rose is an excellent interpreter of cognitive therapy for the lay public. Her writings demonstrate not only an understanding of the therapy but an unusual ability to present complex and technical material in a highly readable and useful way.

In *Woulda/Coulda/Shoulda* the combination of Art Freeman's clinical and technical knowledge and Rose DeWolf's
interpretive skills has produced a therapeutic work that will
provide enormous help to those who now feel blocked by
negative events in their past.

Readers of *Woulda/Coulda/Shoulda* may be interested to
learn how the particular therapeutic approach described in its
pages evolved.

Thirty years ago, I practiced traditional psychoanalytic
psychiatry and conducted research into Freudian theories
and therapy for depression. But the data I developed led
me away from traditional approaches. I found in my research that patients—no matter what their problems—had
a tendency to misread signals from other people. They also
had a number of unreasonable beliefs about themselves and
others. I found that correcting their misinterpretations and
mistaken beliefs made them feel better and helped them to
achieve their goals. It was not necessary to spend a lot of
time talking about childhood material. Focusing on present "here-and-now" problems was usually enough to get
them feeling better in a relatively short period of time. A
number of scientific studies have substantiated this obser-
vation.

The data derived from these studies as well as extensive
clinical experience indicate that people can learn to control
painful mood swings and self-defeating behavior through the
application of a few relatively simple principles and techniques.

Promising results have encouraged the spread of these
techniques. Major centers for cognitive therapy can be found
today across the United States as well as in Norway,
Sweden, Denmark, England, Scotland, Italy, Argentina,
France, Spain, and Portugal. The results have also led to

books such as this one that make information about cognitive therapy available to a broad audience. I believe readers of this book will discover how to achieve greater happiness by overcoming the unhappy focus on the past that Arthur Freeman and Rose DeWolf so aptly call woulda/coulda/shoulda thinking.

CONTENTS

INTRODUCTION

Looking backward—remembering the past—is something everyone does now and again. Sometimes it's just an enjoyable exercise in nostalgia—laughing about an experience in high school, trying to remember all the words to the Beatles song "Yesterday." But sometimes remembering real yesterdays is painful—as we recall an opportunity that was missed or think about an action that turned out to be a terrible mistake.

Few among us have *never* wondered what life might have held for us today if we hadn't taken some action we now regret—if we'd taken this road instead of that one, or if we had acted more boldly when we had the chance.

"If only I'd taken that job that I was offered five years ago, I wouldn't be in this mess I'm in today," you might say to yourself. Or: "If only I'd married John"; or: "If only I'd realized how serious that situation was." Or just: "Where did I go wrong?" With 20-20 hindsight, we discover how very easy it is to go wrong in love, in career—in anything.

For some, this is not a big problem—their wrong turns amount to no more than a few minor chords in a symphony of success. But for others, sour notes struck in the past have had major consequences and continue to reverberate. Some people continue to feel guilty, to feel they have irrevocably "messed up" their lives, to feel they have squandered their resources, to feel victimized by others.

They have succumbed to what can be called "woulda/coulda/shoulda" thinking—that is; continuing, fruitless thoughts about what would have been, what could have been, what should have been if only things had been done differently.

This kind of thinking is immobilizing. People who feel caught in the quagmire of the past have a tendency to "give up" on the future. They find it difficult to galvanize themselves to take an action that might change their lives for the better. They may not even be able to enjoy the good things that already exist in their lives right now.

Consider the following statements. Do any of these apply to *you*?

1. I look at the past and see more failure than success.
2. I would like to change my life, but it's too late now.
3. I believe that if I had handled things differently, I could have had the love I lack today.
4. I just can't get over how somebody I respected misunderstood (or misled, or unfairly treated) me.
5. As long as that person is happy, I can't be.
6. When I make a mistake, it's the kind that follows me to the end of my days.
7. If I knew then what I know now, I'd be more successful in my career.
8. If I knew then what I know now, I'd be half of a happily married couple.
9. I feel guilty about something that happened in my past and I can't get over it.
10. I kick myself for not taking advantage of an opportunity I had years ago. I should have realized that opportunities don't come twice in one lifetime.
11. I feel I have lost status. I spend a lot of time thinking about what I used to have, what I've lost.
12. It seems to me I'm always thinking about the wrong turns I took in the past. I just can't get over what I did. And it gets me down. I feel depressed all the time. I feel hopeless.
13. I'd like to forget what happened but others won't let

me. I can't get away from a constant refrain of "I told you so."

14. I feel I always had the potential for success/love, but I've been dogged by bad luck.

15. I feel I have wasted the best years of my life.

If even one or two of these has a familiar ring, you will find this book helpful to you. Because it explains how to use the techniques of a powerful type of psychotherapy known as cognitive therapy to quiet the echoes of your own personal "sour notes," to cast off the thoughts that hold you in the past, and to enable you to move on to a much fuller life.

Cognitive therapy has been called one of the strongest, if not the strongest, approach in psychotherapy today. This approach was developed by Dr. Aaron T. Beck, a psychiatrist at the University of Pennsylvania, who is now recognized as one of the foremost psychiatric theoreticians in the world today. Not the least of the attractions of cognitive therapy is that it is amazingly easy to understand and to incorporate into one's life. Numerous research studies have proved that it can help those who feel discouraged, deprived, or regretful to develop new hope, new purpose, and new direction.

The chapters of this book describe how destructive woulda/coulda/shoulda thinking develops, and explain in step-by-step fashion how to get free of it. Separate chapters explore specific woulda/coulda/shoulda situations—such as how to break the emotional hold of past love, how to deal with a desire to get even with someone who has hurt you, or how to deal with others in your life who won't let you forget your mistakes.

This book was designed to enable readers to use the techniques of cognitive therapy to find greater satisfaction in the present and to discover new possibilities for the future.

PART 1

*Sending the Past Packing;
Lining Up a New Future*

Chapter One

WOULDA/COULDA/SHOULDA

The sentence usually begins, "If only . . ."

"If only I could live my life—or last week, or yesterday—over again . . ." "If only I knew then what I know now . . ." "If only I had done what I should have done . . ." "If only I'd said the right thing, everything would be different now . . ." And then the sentence ends with, "but it's too late now."

Does this sound familiar? Of course it does. Who among us can claim to have never made a mistake or missed a goal, never regretted a choice we made—or suffered because of someone else's action? Did you marry the wrong person? Take the wrong job? Fail to tell your mom how much you loved her before she died? Recognized opportunity only after you'd let it slide by? Did you goof not once but often? Do you get the feeling that it's become your way of life?

You have lots of company. Most of us can think of stories in our lives with unhappy endings. We know that even the most minuscule of missteps—the mere impulse of a moment—can result in enormous damage. There are many famous examples of that. George Romney was considered a front-runner for the Republican nomination for president of the United States until he made an offhand comment about having been "brainwashed" about America's involvement in Vietnam—and his support vanished. Democrat Edmund Muskie's presidential hopes dissolved in the tears he shed during an emotional response to a vicious editorial attack on his wife.

It's possible to go wrong even when you do what most people would agree is absolutely the "right thing" to do. A good example of that is a story about a young man who was invited to join a lottery pool.

It seems that there was, that week, a prize of $28 million to be won in a Pennsylvania state lottery game. Five friends who worked together talked about chipping in ten dollars apiece to buy tickets together, with an agreement to share the prize if any of their tickets won. Four of the five agreed to put up ten dollars. But the fifth declined. He said he had better uses for his money. Everybody knows (and it *is* statistically true) that you are more likely to be hit by lightning than to win a multimillion-dollar lottery jackpot. Most people would agree the young man was only being sensible—except that, in this instance, his buddies had the winning ticket.

And did he kick himself when he found out . . . when he thought about the $5.8 million that would have been his share had he chipped in only ten dollars? What do you think?

The real question, however, is not whether he kicked himself for refusing to join the pool and not whether he will occasionally shake his head about it in the future, but rather whether he will *continually* kick himself over that perfectly reasonable omission for the rest of his life. Will the thought of what he woulda/coulda/shoulda been able to afford poison all the pleasure of what he *can* afford?

THE MINEFIELD OF LIFE

It comes down to this: When you walk through a minefield, you are bound to step wrong now and again. And sometimes life can seem very much like a field sowed all around with explosive mines.

You agree to sign a contract without reading the small print because you believe you are dealing with someone who is honest and seems to answer your questions quite openly. But later you become a little anxious. Maybe you acted too quickly. Maybe you should have checked. And it turns out you have indeed signed your way into a costly, complicated mess.

Or, you felt you couldn't ask that wonderful woman for a date because she is very tall and you know she wouldn't go out with you because you are 5' 5". And then she marries somebody 5' 3". Every time you see her now, you wonder what life would be like if you'd been braver.

Or, you marry Charlie even though your mother thinks he is a bum, your sister thinks he is insensitive, your friends say he is a bore, your minister says he is no good, and, alas, it turns out your mother, sister, friends, and minister were right. If only you had listened . . .

Or, you don't hit it off with the new boss, and as a result you are given worthless assignments. The injustice of this makes you seethe. You can't help complaining, even though you know that this only makes your co-workers uncomfortable. You know that constantly thinking about what he *should* have done and what you *could* have done aren't helping matters, but . . .

You might feel you have failed to prevent harm from coming to someone you love. Or brought harm upon yourself by failing to take advantage of opportunities that came your way. Or maybe this feeling of woulda/coulda/shoulda sweeps over you when you bump into someone you knew way back when who seems to be much more successful than you are. You can't put your finger on where you went wrong—but you are certain you did.

Or it could be that someone close to you seems determined to foist that conclusion upon you. Someone tells you that if you had only listened to him or her, or done things this or that way, you could have, would have, and should have accomplished more.

There is no shortage of mines to step on. There is no shortage of ways to "go wrong."

HOW WE REACT TO MISTAKES

People differ greatly in the way they deal with that sense of having gone wrong. We know that some people are able just to shrug off their mistakes (perhaps much too easily). And some people seem to have an ability to turn any adversity into a strength. For them, even the most terrible catastrophe is merely a learning experience. But most of us fall somewhere in between—we have to struggle to come to terms with the wrong turn we have taken on the path of life.

You undoubtedly know how difficult that struggle can be. It's hard to get your mind off a major misstep or mistake. It's hard to *stop* thinking about how it might have been avoided. It's hard to *start* thinking about anything else. It's frustrating. It can be paralyzing. It's like trying to walk while looking back over your shoulder. It's like trying to run in foot-deep wet concrete.

We call this constant sense of regret woulda/coulda/shoulda thinking. People who seek professional help for this form of unhappiness don't necessarily define their need for relief in exactly that way. Most simply say they are depressed or in a constant state of anxiety. They will say they just can't function anymore. Or they will say, "All I know is that I'm very unhappy." But when woulda/coulda/shoulda thinking is the problem, that fact quickly surfaces. We know when what is bothering us are mistakes, missteps, or missed opportunities.

Woulda/coulda/shoulda thinkers cannot describe their feelings without using the past tense. Phrases like this are very common:

—"I keep thinking of what I did. I'm exhausted thinking about it, but I can't stop. I feel so bad, I can't get on with my life."
—"I feel I've wasted my life. I had a chance, and I muffed it."
—"I play that scene with Larry over and over again in my head. I just can't forget it."
—"It wasn't supposed to turn out like this. I keep thinking of all the dumb things I did that got me where I am today."
—"I can't sleep at night. I keep seeing myself in that situation. I'm so afraid of having this happen to me again. I keep thinking about what I could have done or should have done. And I don't want my whole life to be like this."

HOW WOULDA/COULDA/SHOULDA THINKING DEVELOPS

No one should have to endure a lifetime of woulda/coulda/shoulda thinking. Because it is something that we learn—and, in most cases, can unlearn.

Looking back on your mistakes is something you are taught to do as a child. You get into trouble, as all kids do—

maybe you broke a friend's toy or dropped ink on the new living-room rug, or you said something that hurt your sister's feelings—and Mom sits you down and says sternly, "You just stay there awhile and think about what you did."

Thinking about what you did is a valuable learning experience. That is how we learn to be tactful, to be careful, to be civilized. If we never reviewed our mistakes, we would just keep making them. If we never thought about the consequences of our actions, chaos and cruelty would multiply. Undoubtedly, that is why many religions place great importance on meditating on one's sins. That is why the courts deal so sternly with offenders who show no signs of remorse. *Never* thinking of a wrong you have done is a sign of mental illness. When psychologist Zygmont Piotrowski studied psychopathic murderers, he found their most common characteristic was a total absence of guilt—that is, they *never* gave a thought to the effect of their crime.

But although there is no doubt that it's a good idea to look back and reflect on your mistakes from time to time, it is *not* a good idea to continue to review those mistakes over and over and over again. We all know that it's possible to overdo a good thing—you can improve your health by making sure that your daily diet includes all the recommended amounts of vitamins, but you may harm yourself if you swallow vitamin pills in excessive amounts. In the same way, helpful thinking about past mistakes can turn into harmful woulda/coulda/shoulda thinking. Mere reflection becomes endless concentration. Thinking about a past mistake or hurt or missed opportunity becomes not being able to *stop* thinking about it.

The term most often used for this kind of thinking is "rumination." Cows ruminate when they chew their food—that is, they chew the same material over and over again. They even bring back material they've swallowed to give it still another going over. This suits the cow's digestive system very well. But when people bring back events of the past to mentally chew them over again and again, they do themselves a great deal of harm.

It's hard to say why some of us learn to look back just long enough to learn a lesson, and some of us learn to look back at so much greater length. It may be a matter of how you have interpreted the admonitions of your religion. It may be a matter of how strongly your parents emphasized "thinking about what you've done." Or you may have been influenced in a much subtler manner. You may have observed your mother, father, aunt, or grandmother going through a woulda/coulda/shoulda litany and, as a child, automatically assumed that this was reasonable adult behavior. There is no way for a child to know that it is unreasonable. Thus, if there were woulda/coulda/shoulda thinkers in your family, you may have grown up simply following their example.

"WHY" IS NOT IMPORTANT

This may sound like heresy, but the fact is that knowing *why* your mind gets stuck in mud when it travels backward is not necessary in order to make major changes in *how* you respond. Think of having a piece of sand in your eye. It's incredibly irritating. But the worst thing about it is that it prevents you from seeing where you are going. Would you waste time worrying about *why* that piece of sand was in the air or *why* it picked your eye to land in, or would you take immediate steps simply to get it out so that you could get moving again?

Some of those who have learned how to get moving again at the Center for Cognitive Therapy say that they had to be prodded into coming. They had already "tried therapy," they said. And it hadn't worked. They didn't see what "more therapy" would do. What they learned was that cognitive therapy is not "more"—it is "different," and that this different therapy is particularly suited to dealing with the woulda/coulda/shoulda problem. Traditional psychotherapy takes an archeological view that requires digging through and reviewing the past—and this is not helpful if the reason you are unhappy is that you are already reviewing the past too often. Expeditions into your past relationships might help you to better understand why certain events in your life occurred—and yet still not put an end to your suffering. If you have sought the help of a traditional therapist in trying to get your life out of the woulda/coulda/shoulda trap, you know this is true.

WHAT NEXT, NOT WHY

Cognitive therapy is different because it is active—that is, it involves doing things, not just talking about them. It focuses on attaining specific goals that are set as much by the patient as by the therapist. It is different because it works in a remarkably short period of time—in months rather than years. And—of particular importance to woulda/coulda/shoulda thinkers—it is different because it asks the question "What next?" rather than "Why?"

Whatever has happened, has happened. If an opportunity has been missed, then it's gone. And dwelling on it will not bring it back again. In fact, you know from experience that dwelling on it is preventing you from experiencing pleasure in the present or moving toward greater comfort in the future. Thinking about what went wrong and why it went wrong leads to inaction—to giving up and giving in. Thinking about what can be put right, what can be done now, what new opportunities can be developed, leads to action, to change, to hope, to a new attitude about life's possibilities.

But as you undoubtedly know, it isn't enough simply to say, "Think positive thoughts!" Or, "Just forget about it." Or, "Cheer up. Everything will be fine." Developing a new perspective on life requires much more than a few well-meaning phrases. It requires a knowledge of how people develop self-defeating patterns of thought—and how those patterns can be changed. That's where cognitive therapy comes in. The word *cognitive* comes from the Latin word for "thinking" or "perception."

Numerous research studies have shown that when people are upset, they are very likely to start thinking in negative, harmful ways that they *aren't even aware of.* Here's a very basic example of thought processes gone awry that might occur to . . . say, a businessman . . . who gets stuck in traffic en route to the airport. "Oh no, I'm going to miss my plane," he says. And then his mind starts racing. "If I miss the plane, I'll miss the meeting. If I miss the meeting, I'll lose the client. If I lose this client, I'll lose my job. If I lose this job, I'll never find another. I might as well be dead. . . ." These thoughts come so quickly, so *automatically,* the man doesn't really notice them. What he does notice is that he feels just terrible. He is sweating. His stomach is tight. His head is starting to pound. And all of this is happening to him even though *he hasn't actually missed the plane!* Not yet anyway. For all he knows, he'll still get there in time. Or the flight may be delayed. Besides, even if he does miss the flight, will that really mean the loss of client, job, and entire career? Not likely. If he were *aware* of what he is thinking, he'd know he is exaggerating the situation.

Thinking about a mistake of the past can, in a similar manner, unleash dozens, even hundreds, of negative thoughts just below the level of awareness. When you think, "If only I had done such-and-such, I would be happy today," you don't stop there. Like a flock of startled birds, secondary thoughts start automatically flitting across your mind: "I should have known better." "I was stupid." "I'm always doing something stupid." "Everything I do is stupid." "Everyone thinks I'm stupid." "I'll never get anywhere." "There's nothing I can do." "I've ruined my life. I'm such a jerk." And on and on and on, while your stomach knots up and your heart seems to be turning to ice. Who wouldn't feel sick, facing such an attack? Who wouldn't feel discouraged?

Yet, more likely than not, these attacks are unfair and un-substantiated. You are probably being harder on yourself than you would ever be on someone else. You are, like the busi-nessman on the way to the airport, exaggerating—even though those exaggerations only make you feel worse—which leads to even more dismal thoughts, more discouraging con-clusions.

To change this situation, you must become aware of what you are thinking—and *how* what you are thinking affects your mood and behavior. That is where cognitive therapy can help you. The aim of cognitive therapy is to make unspoken thoughts spoken. It teaches us how to listen to ourselves, how to recognize thoughts that are exaggerated, unfair, or just plain wrong. It provides the tools we need to become advocates for ourselves.

In succeeding chapters, we will describe the techniques of cognitive therapy and provide exercises that will enable you to make full use of its powerful psychological tools. But for now, let us merely restate the important point that even though you cannot erase a setback or loss that has already occurred, you *can* change the influence that any given setback or loss has on your life. You do this by understanding your own thought processes.

HOW PEOPLE SET THEMSELVES UP FOR
WOULDA/COULDA/SHOULDA SITUATIONS

Here's an example of a very simple, very common thought process that gets us into lots of trouble—not just at moments of special stress, but all the time. Let's call it the "Life Equation."

We all learned equations back in first grade (or was it second grade?), when the teacher explained that $4 + 5 = 9$. We also learned that $7 + 1 = 8$ and $4 + 3 = 7$. We learned that the scientific way of solving a problem is to assess all the information on the left-hand side of the equation before attempting to set down an answer on the right:

$$2 + 2 = ?$$
$$2 + 2 = 4$$

We also learned that different combinations of numbers on the left can yield the exact same result on the right:

$$3 + 6 = 9$$
$$4 + 5 = 9$$
$$8 + 1 = 9$$

As we grow up, we discover that life has its equations, too. And we learn to tote up life experiences and come up with a result, in ways very much like those we learned in beginning arithmetic.

For instance: A young man goes to a singles bar, spots a young woman who looks interesting. He smiles in her direction. She smiles back. Now, he waves in her direction. She waves back. Aha. Those are the "numbers" on the left-hand side of the equation. And what do they add up to? She's interested.

However, there are times that you find yourself in a mental
state in which you gloomily cast scientific method aside and,
instead of adding up your life experiences to arrive at a total,
you *start with the total* and then juggle your life experiences to
equal that result.

You quite accurately point out that there are many different combinations that equal nine, but then leap from there
to a determination that *every* combination in your life will
also equal nine. . . .

Suppose the young man in the singles bar had decided
before he ever got there that he is a loser. He'd already concluded, based on some unfortunate experiences in the past,
that no woman could possibly be interested in him. So, although he has reluctantly agreed to go to the bar with some
friends, he "knows" that for him this outing will amount to
"nothing." And what happens is that he mentally adjusts
every component part of that evening's experience to get the
result he expects. When the young woman smiles, he assumes she is smiling at someone else. When she waves, she is
only being polite.

He will do whatever mental calculations are required to
ensure that his Life Equation reaches the total he has pre-
determined. He'll deliberately add the numbers incorrectly if
he has to, or he'll manipulate the numbers if that's what it
takes. If he has a life experience equivalent to 100, he'll manage to think up some kind of negative that can be subtracted
from it so that he'll get back to the result he expects.

That's how it works. If you flatly decide, "I have taken the
wrong turn in life *and there is no way out*," you, too, are
determining the result of your equation in advance. If every
scientist did things this way, we would still be living in
caves and trying to figure out how to get a fire started. Of
course, you cannot ignore what has gone before, but that
doesn't mean it should forever stand in the way of your future.

ARGUING YOUR DEFENSE

That means learning how to do a better job of analyzing the data of your life before drawing conclusions from it. A lawyer might put it this way: You have to learn to argue a defense. Lawyers go to law school to learn the techniques and strategies of arguing a defense in court; you will be learning techniques and strategies of arguing a defense in your mind.

What if there really were a court in which we were judged for all the goofs we make as we go through life? Suppose, for example, that you stood accused of "unforgivable stupidity" for failing to succeed at some particular endeavor or for saying something so foolish that it brought a budding relationship to an abrupt and unnecessary end.

The "prosecution" has lined up ninety witnesses to testify against you. And on top of that, the "stupidity police" have your signed confession. After the prosecuting attorney rests his case, your attorney stands up to speak a few words. Only a few. "Ladies and gentlemen of the jury," says your defender, "despite what you have heard, my client is a nice person." The defense then rests.

What do you suppose will be the jury's verdict? What do you think are your chances of winning an acquittal? Anywhere from zero to none, right? The jury will not only declare you guilty, it will undoubtedly recommend a life sentence. Now, consider this scenario: After the ninety witnesses testify for the prosecution, the defense introduces its star witness: Mother Teresa. She testifies that on the night you are accused of unforgivable stupidity, you were having dinner with her and Pope John Paul II. She contends that what the prosecutor says about you could not actually have happened. If you confessed, it was either because you were coerced or confused. The pope has offered to take the stand if necessary.

What is your chance of acquittal now? About 100 percent? The jury will not only free you; they will probably offer to take you to lunch!

Final and most likely scenario: The prosecution is able to produce ninety witnesses over a period of seven days who testify against you, but your attorney has managed to assemble fifty witnesses who testify on your behalf over a period of four days. They describe your state of mind when the incident occurred. They talk of mitigating factors. They explain the events that led up to the "crime." They testify to other events of your life that show you in a better light.

What are your chances now? Surely, at least fifty—fifty— even though the prosecution witnesses outnumber yours. And why is that? Simply because your witnesses enable the jury to hear the other side of the story. And having heard it, they may just decide in your favor. They may decide that what you did wasn't so stupid after all. They may decide that even if it was stupid, it was hardly "unforgivable." They may decide you deserve a second chance.

Our goal in these pages is to enable you to present a defense to the jury that lives in your brain. If you are able to argue a defense to the worst charges you hurl at yourself, you may decide to acquit yourself entirely—or at least let yourself off with a light sentence.

When you look at your past and can only think, "I missed out on the one chance I've had or ever will have," or "I made a mistake that can never be put right," you are pleading guilty without benefit of a fair trial. If you never consider any rebuttal, any alternative explanation, or any possible defense, then you will have given yourself a life sentence of misery.

Rarely is such a sentence deserved. Most likely, you are entitled to a fairer kind of justice than you are meting out. What you need is a saw hidden in the middle of a cake. And it is the intention of this book to bring it to you.

A NEW DIRECTION

Making use of that "saw" involves more than simply agreeing that you *want* to put your past behind you. It means taking some very specific steps to accomplish that result.

There's an old story about a man who prays to God every day to let him win the lottery. But ten years go by, and he has never won a dime. Frustrated, he gets down on his knees, holds his arms up to the heavens, and cries, "My God, why have you abandoned me? Have I not led a good life? Have I not prayed for your help twice a day, every single day for the past ten years? Why have you never once answered my prayers? Why have I not won even a tiny prize in the lottery?" And lo, a light appears all around, and from somewhere far away a voice calls down to him. The voice says, "Joe . . . Joe . . . I hear you. I have heard all of your prayers. I know you are a good man. But, Joe, give me a break. Buy a ticket."

You have to buy a ticket. You have to make an effort. But it doesn't take an *enormous* effort. Changing negative thought patterns is much easier than most people think. It is not uncommon for a client at the Cognitive Therapy Center to say, I can't believe this will work for me. Because I'm in deep, deep trouble . . . I'm in such misery . . . I am so depressed. This much suffering can't possibly be relieved just by learning some new ways to analyze my problems. . . ."

Yes, it can.

Have you ever seen a giant 747 airplane arrive at an airport? The huge behemoth lands and taxis up to the gate, where a ground crewman stands ready to throw a couple of wooden blocks, no bigger than fireplace logs, in front and back of each of the 747's wheels. What do these little blocks do? They keep that enormous plane from rolling. Amazing but true, the blocks that keep human beings from rolling are usually just as small, comparatively speaking, as the blocks under the wheels of the 747. Those blocks would not keep the 747 from moving if its engines were powered up, of course. And humans, too, can get out of "park" if they simply learn how to switch on their power. The techniques you will be learning in the following chapters will enable you to power up—to get moving . . . to bump over the blocks . . . and move ahead.

Moving ahead doesn't mean forgetting where you've been. It means acknowledging that where you've been is not the only place you can go.

Chapter Two:

TAKING A MORE REALISTIC
LOOK AT YOUR LIFE

In the Mel Brooks movie *Blazing Saddles* there is a scene that perfectly captures the woulda/coulda/shoulda dilemma. The good guys are being chased across the desert by the bad guys. And the bad guys are gaining on them. The good guys have to figure out a way to slow the bad guys down. And what do they do?

They set up a tollbooth. The toll is a nickel. The bad guys gallop up to the tollbooth and realize they don't have enough nickels to pay their way through. So they send one of their number back to town to get change. And while they wait impatiently for him to return with the nickels, the good guys get away.

Of course, it's totally ridiculous. A tollbooth in the middle of the desert? From our seats in the movie theater we can laugh at the bad guys, because we realize, as they do not, how easy it would be simply to ride around this silly booth. They could ride through it without paying the toll. Who would stop them?

You can just imagine what they are thinking: "Darn, a tollbooth, just as we were about to catch up with them. If only we'd thought to bring nickels. . . . I should have known there might be a tollbooth here. If I hadn't bought coffee this morning, I would have had a nickel with me and been halfway to Denver by now. But now I'll just have to wait until somebody comes along and gives me a nickel. Although the way my luck has been going lately, by the time I get the nickel, the toll will have gone up to ten cents. . . ."

This scene strikes a chord with moviegoers because it's such a perfect parody of human nature. Some people spend their whole lives accepting every tollbooth that rises before them without ever questioning whether it has any right to be there, or looking to see if there is a way around it, or considering whether, on this occasion, it might be best to ignore it. Some people never think ahead to the possibility that a tollbooth *might* arise on the road, and so bring some extra change along. And some spend so much time planning ahead for every imaginable kind of road barrier, they never get around to actually setting out on a journey.

The scene is an apt metaphor for the problem of woulda/coulda/shoulda thinking, because the tollbooth is real. It's not a mirage. It's there. Just as whatever you regret about your past life is real—the mistake, the missed opportunity, the failure to capitalize on success, the feeling that somewhere along the line you got off the train before it was in the station. And what we can easily see from our vantage point in the movie theater is that what is keeping the pursuers back is not the *reality* of that booth, but rather the way they are *thinking* about it.

They are so focused on the *barrier* that the tollbooth presents that they don't see all those miles and miles of open desert on either side of it. They are so focused on the rules they associate with proper tollbooth behavior that they automatically accept them, even though we can see that, in this instance, it's a silly thing to do.

Suppose, to digress to real life for a minute, you have cut yourself badly and have to get to a hospital. On the way you come to an unmanned tollbooth for which you do not have the proper coin. Would you just sit around bleeding to death, lamenting the fact that you had not thought to take a different route, or would you drive right on through and mail the toll to the proper authorities later?

Obviously, the bad guys in *Blazing Saddles* aren't thinking too clearly. Of course, they are stressed. They've had a long day. And on top of that, they have never learned to analyze how they are thinking about their dilemma.

HOW YOU THINK AFFECTS THE WAY YOU FEEL

Analyzing what you are thinking lies at the core of cognitive therapy, because how we think affects how we feel and how we behave. When we perceive events as shameful or threatening, we tend to feel defeated, deprived, depressed or anxious. Our insides seem to be tied up in knots. That can lead to crying, to avoiding people, and to avoiding activities.

Yet very often when we make those judgments that tangle our insides and inhibit action, we are not "thinking straight," but rather distorting reality in some way. Distorting reality doesn't mean being "crazy." The men who can't see their way around the tollbooth are not severely disturbed. They have simply allowed the situation they face to get the better of their common sense. This is something we all do at times.

Here is a "distortion of reality" that many will find familiar:

Julie had barely made it to her desk one Tuesday morning when the telephone rang and she heard her secretary say, "Pete's on the line."

"Uh-oh," Julie says to herself. "This means trouble." She knows what this call is about. Pete is going to ask for the Bartlett report, which Julie had said would be ready today. But the Bartlett report doesn't exist—yet. All Julie has to offer so far are excuses. And Pete is not one to listen to excuses calmly. Julie can feel her stomach going into tuck position as she reaches for the phone. She is thinking, "What does the man want from me? Does he think I don't have other things to do?" Aloud into the phone, she says only, "Pete, hi . . . what can I do for you?"

And Pete replies, "Mornin', Julie. I called to ask for a favor. Mary Ellen Chase from marketing says Herb Vincent has applied for an opening she's got over there, and she's looking for a recommendation. You know Herb well. Would you be willing to give her a call? . . . . Thanks a lot. One more thing. Marv just got a call from the Bartlett people postponing our meeting—again. I think we can forget about that bunch for a while. That won't make you unhappy, will it? I know you've got more than enough on your plate as it is."

Is there anybody in the world who hasn't had that kind of experience? Your mind tells you what is going to happen. You can see it happen. You can hear it happen. Your nerve endings and stomach can *feel* it happen. But it doesn't happen. Not even close.

Here is another example:

Diane and Jim pass each other in the hallway. Diane smiles and cheerily says hello. But Jim doesn't even seem to notice her. He strides past quickly as if she weren't there at all. Diane turns and watches him go. "What a creep!" she fumes. "What a snob! I'm good enough for him when he needs some sucker to help him finish his work. But I'm not worth three seconds of his valuable time to say hello. That . . ."

Along comes Rita, who stops to tell Diane that Jim just got a call informing him that his father has been rushed to the hospital in critical condition. "Poor guy," says Rita, "he looked numb. I asked him if he wanted me to drive him there, but . . ."

"Oh."

Is Jim still "a creep"? Of course not.

Obviously, what's going on in both of these examples is that very popular activity known as jumping to the wrong conclusion, which is just one of many ways we distort reality in our thoughts.

BENDING REALITY IN A POSITIVE WAY

It is only fair to say that it is possible to bend reality in positive as well as negative ways, and that sometimes people who fool themselves are better off for it. Football coaches are a good example: "This team is tough. You guys [all ninety-pound weaklings] are going to go out there and push those wimps on the other team [each one 7' tall, 290 pounds] all over the field. They haven't got a chance." And it could be that the weaklings get so fired up with determination (while the other side is having an off day) that they win. Similarly, a certain amount of unfounded belief in oneself can be the key to major business success. This is not to say that positive distortion cannot get you into trouble. If you feel pains in your chest and down your arm but decide to ignore them because you say, "I'm too young to have a heart attack," you may not get much older. But the fact is that the distortions that tend to cause us the most grief are the negative ones. This book concentrates on negative errors in thinking, because they lie at the core of woulda/coulda/shoulda problems.

BREAKING THE NEGATIVE DISTORTION HABIT

Both Julie, who thought the boss was going to be angry at her, and Diane, who thought Jim was snubbing her, were quite aware of the conclusions they were drawing—even if they weren't aware their conclusions were wrong. But as we saw in Chapter One, it is possible for misery-making thoughts to race through your mind so quickly you aren't even fully aware of them. You are aware only of their effect— feeling low, feeling uptight, feeling out of control. This is most likely to happen if, because of stressful situations in the past, you have gotten into the *habit* of thinking in ways that tend to assume "the worst."

Maybe you have never associated the word *habit* with the way you think. Most of us tend to think of a habit as a physical action—usually a negative one, like smoking or biting one's nails. But a habit is simply something a person does without consciously concentrating on it—like turning a doorknob, or putting your foot on the brake when you come to a red light. Although someone else may notice that you always pull on the doorknob to make sure you've locked the door, you may do it so automatically that you yourself don't even realize the action is taking place. Most of the very basic things we do every day—the way we get out of bed in the morning, the way we walk, talk, wash, whatever—we do out of habit. And life is made easier because of it. If we didn't have habits, we'd go crazy. We'd have to concentrate on every move we make.

And just as we develop habits of action, we develop habits of thinking, too—habits that once developed become almost as natural as breathing. For example, you may know somebody who tends to say things like, "You *never* listen to me," or "This *always* happens to me." This is a person who makes a habit of sweeping generalizations. After all, how many things really *never* happen or *always* happen? Many of us tend to find this kind of comment annoying, and yet the person saying it probably does not realize just how often he or she thinks—and speaks—in that way.

If you want to change a habit, you must first make yourself aware of it. If you want to stop biting your nails, you have to consciously pay attention to that action—so that you can stop it. So it is with bad habits of thinking. Woulda/coulda/shoulda thinking is a habit. It's a pattern of thinking that is only too easy to fall into when confronted with a distressing situation. Woulda/coulda/shoulda thinking is not a single thought—but rather a combination of thinking errors. The specific combination may be different for different individuals.

COMMON MISTAKES OF THE MIND

How can the thinking process go awry? Let us count just some of the ways. The errors of thinking described in the following list are common to all of us, and have the potential for causing enormous damage when they become our *primary way* of relating to the world.

Describing and putting a name to errors of thinking make it easier to recognize them when they pop up in our thinking. It's somewhat like having a neighbor ask you what you think about the new yellow curtains she has hung in her upstairs window. You might well reply, "What curtains?" You may have passed that house a dozen times, but you didn't notice them. Your mind was on other things. However, once those curtains have been *called to your attention,* you are very likely to notice them the next time you pass by.

In similar fashion, once you are aware of all the ways we distort reality when we are upset, you can begin searching for them among those thoughts that fly through your mind when you are upset. You can then begin the process of changing negative thinking habits into more positive ones.

1. All-or-Nothing Thinking

This is the belief that if you don't have it all, you have nothing. Something is either black or white, good or bad. If you don't win, you have lost *everything*. You are having all-or-nothing thoughts when you say, "If I didn't do it before, I can't do it ever." Or, "I didn't get to be president of the company at age forty, therefore I'm a total failure."

Sandy had personal problems during her freshman year at college and fell behind in her work. Finally, she felt she had no choice but to drop all five courses for which she had registered. "I'll start fresh next year," she said. But, instead, Sandy took a job. She was happy to be earning money at first, but now, at thirty-one, she finds herself frustrated and wishing desperately that she'd completed college. "If I could have stayed in school when I was younger, everything would be different today," she says, "but it's too late now. If I started now, I'd be thirty-five when I graduated."

Sandy is an all-or-nothing thinker. It may well be that Sandy did not have to drop out of *all* her courses when she did. She had fallen behind in five, and so gave up on five. But she might have been able to talk to the professors involved and to arrange to complete the work of at least two or three of them. That would have kept her in school. By deciding it was all or nothing, Sandy set herself up for a missed opportunity.

And she is doing it *again* at age thirty-one. By deciding that one must go to college at eighteen or *never*, she will miss the opportunity to achieve the goal that a college degree would make possible. It is true that Sandy would be thirty-five years old by the time she earns a degree, but in four years she will be thirty-five whether she goes to school or not. If she gets the degree she craves, she might be more cheerful at thirty-five than she is now. And she will not have to ponder what woulda/coulda/shoulda happened in her life if only she'd made the effort.

2. Perfectionism

A close relative of all-or-nothing thinking is perfectionism, the belief that if you do not perform perfectly, you will be embarrassed, disgraced, and doomed. This one gets people into enormous amounts of trouble, since it is really quite difficult to be perfect 100 percent of the time. Not being able to do something perfectly can end up meaning not doing it at all.

Bob had been pretty excited when he was assigned to come up with a new marketing plan for his division. If he did a good job, it would be noticed. Bob worked pretty hard on the plan, but nothing he put on paper pleased him. Nothing seemed good enough. The deadline for turning in the plan came and went. Not only didn't he do a good job, he didn't do any job at all.

Bob may say to himself afterward, "I could have done it. But I didn't have enough time." Or, "I should have turned in the plan I developed. It probably would have been fine." Yet he must acknowledge either way that not having turned in the plan has undermined his standing with the company.

Perfectionism can undermine you in another way. It can rob you of pleasure even when you do perform well.

Suppose Bob is a member of a baseball team that wins a league championship. He is rightly proud of himself and his teammates for that achievement. But then the team is defeated by the champs of a rival league in the series that determines which team gets possession of the interleague championship trophy.

Bob's team has gone from being Number One to Number Two. To the perfectionists among the team's fans, this means the team members are "bums." And Bob feels that way himself. He feels like a loser. He could have played better, he tells himself. "If only I'd done a better job of fielding." Other members of Bob's team also wish that they'd won— but they are still able to feel the satisfaction of being first in their own league. They say, "Wait till next year." But Bob feels that losing the trophy is losing *everything*.

There is a difference between thinking positively—"I'm

going to do a great job." Or, "I'm going to practice until I
get it right"—and saying, "I cannot fail, because if I do, I'm
a totally worthless human."

3. Overgeneralization

This means taking a single event and generalizing it to all
events. If it happened once, it will always happen.

Debbie, who hoped for a career as a writer, submitted an
article she felt she'd done a very good job on to the editor of
a local magazine. A week later, the article came back in the
mail along with a form letter from the editor saying, in
effect, thank you but no. After that, Debbie couldn't bring
herself to try again. Not with that editor, or with any other.
"If only I'd done a better job," she said to herself. "I guess I
don't have what it takes. Editors don't like my stuff."

Editors? There was just one editor of one magazine making
a judgment (maybe not even the right judgment) about one
article. But Debbie accepts this single judgment as represent-
ing every editor in the world saying she is no good.

How easy it is for "I tried it once and it didn't work" to
become "There is no point in trying, because it can't work."
Instead of torturing herself by endless imagining of what
woulda/coulda/shoulda happened if that single article had
been accepted, Debbie should join a writer's organization so
she can listen to tales other writers tell about how many rejection slips they collected before finally selling their first,
second and ninety-sixth pieces.

4. Global Labeling

This one is a variation on overgeneralization. It is saying, "I
can't do anything right. Nothing ever works out for me." It
is not only saying, "I didn't sell this article to the editor,

therefore no article I will ever write on any subject can possibly sell"—but also saying, "Since I didn't succeed in selling this article I wrote, that means I can't succeed in *anything*." It is often said that no one can be as hard on you as you . . . and it's true.

Yet, objectively, we would have to conclude that if Debbie had not already succeeded in doing some things—getting the article written, mailing it to the magazine—that editor would never have gotten a chance to turn it down. It is not true that since she could not sell that article, she must accept the label of loser in every facet of life.

5. Catastrophizing

There are two components to catastrophizing. One is that old favorite "making a mountain out of a molehill." You magnify the potential results of any misstep. Remember the businessman we described in Chapter One who thought he was going to miss his plane? This is what he was doing. He magnified the mere possibility of missing an airplane into the destruction of his career. The second component of catastrophizing is hopeless capitulation when a true catastrophe strikes—a thought process that might go something like this: "I've lost my job, and I'll never find another. There is no point in looking. I know there's nothing out there. I'm nothing without a job. There is no point in going on."

Catastrophizing is common in woulda/coulda/shoulda thinking. "If only I'd taken that offer from the Jones Corporation, I'd be a vice-president now. But when I turned that offer down, I ruined my life. I see that now. And it's too late to do anything about it." Even if it was a mistake to reject the Jones offer, even if it is too late to do anything about that *specific* job opportunity now, is it reasonable to conclude that

it is also too late for any and all other options? Evidence
abounds that this is rarely, if ever, so.

6. Minimizing

Minimizing occurs when you don't give yourself credit for
paying proper attention to a decision when that decision
turns out to be wrong. It also occurs when you, in fact, don't
pay proper attention to important events.

Here's an example of the first variety:

Nancy left a good job for what she thought was a better one.
She'd checked with other people at the new firm and had
satisfied herself that the opportunity she sought was there. But
unknown to Nancy—and, indeed, to the majority of those
who worked for this company—the owners had decided to sell
it to a rival firm. When that sale occurred, Nancy was among
those laid off as the new firm consolidated operations. Nancy
berated herself for being "stupid" in taking the new job. "I
should have known this would happen," she said. But the
disappointment Nancy suffered had nothing to do with being
"stupid." She did not give herself credit for making what
seemed to be a sensible choice at the time.

Minimizing also occurs when you *don't* pay proper attention to big events. Joe has a paper due on Wednesday. He
knows full well that this particular paper counts heavily toward his final grade and that final grade will count heavily in
the decision over whether or not he gets accepted to graduate
school. But he prefers not to think about it. "I have plenty of
time," says Joe. "I'll do it Tuesday night." But on Tuesday
night Joe finds that all the books he needs to consult for this
paper have been checked out and aren't due back for weeks.
"Oh no," says Joe, "I should have come in earlier. By minimizing what is really important to him, Joe is digging himself into a woulda/coulda/shoulda pit.

7. Comparative Thinking

We live in a society in which we are taught from an early age to compare ourselves to others. "Look how nicely little Robert is playing. Why can't you play quietly like that?" "Your cousin Kathy got all 'A's on her report card. If you applied yourself, you could get 'A's too." We soon learn to notice who has more, who is bigger, who is better. This competition is not always a bad thing, unless, in making your comparisons, you find that you never, ever measure up. Others are all happier, worthier, more famous, more successful.

John feels a cloud of gloom descend on him when he reads in the paper that Ed, who used to work in his office, has just been named vice-president of a computer-technology firm in California. John has never felt like such a failure. Ed left John's office five years ago. John thinks, "I could have left then, too. I should have left. What a jerk I am. That's the story of my whole life."

John draws his conclusions about Ed's relative success even though he really doesn't know much about Ed's life or the firm for which Ed now works. By assuming that whatever Ed has is better than what he has—or could get—or that Ed got his position by marrying the boss's daughter, John closes the door on future action on his own behalf. And by assuming that the whole world is comparing him—negatively—to Ed, he opens the door to depression or anxiety.

8. Uncritical Acceptance of the Critics

We define our own self-worth by what others think of us. Athletes have to put up with fans booing them from time to time. When you hit a home run, you are a hero—when you strike out, you are a bum. Baseball players learn that they can't let the criticism immobilize them or they'll never get a chance to hit the home run.

Obviously, some criticism is warranted. There is an old saying that if three people tell you that you look drunk, perhaps you'd best sit down. We learn from listening to the criticism of others—but listening does not mean accepting all criticism as equally valid.

Mary's favorite professor at college told her she had the talent to write the Great American Novel. When he hears that Mary has written—and sold—a romantic novel, he is furious with her. "You are wasting your life," he tells her. "You are degrading the talent God gave you. I'm ashamed of you." Until then, Mary had been proud of what she'd done. She didn't call it great literature—but she thought it was pleasant reading. She had enjoyed writing it. She had enjoyed being paid for it. Now, she was embarrassed to put her name on it. "I should never have done that," she moans. "I'm a failure. I've disappointed someone who had faith in me."

But is there some law that says that writing enjoyable fluff forever bars you from writing "literature"? And will Mary actually be happier living the life the professor envisions for her than living the one she had been enjoying? Is Mary a failure just because this professor says so? These are the kinds of questions we must learn to ask ourselves when we hear criticism. Because not all criticism is equally valid.

There may be critics in your life who will never, ever be pleased, no matter what you do. ("Look, Ma, I got six 'A's and one 'B' on my report card." "Why did you get a 'B,' weren't you paying attention?") No matter what you do, some people will find a way to say, "Yes, but . . ."

"I got a new car." "Yes, but it's not a Rolls-Royce." "I'm the president of the company." "Yes, but the company is not AT&T." "Hasn't this been an enjoyable visit?" "Yes, but you don't visit me often enough." These are people who try to pressure you into feeling as if you woulda/coulda/shoulda done more or better, no matter how much or how well you've done.

If you are already feeling negative about yourself, negative comments can plunge you into despair. That is why you must ask, "Who is telling me this? How reliable is this critic?"

9. Selective Editing

Imagine a scientist who analyzes water and notices only the hydrogen atoms but not the oxygen, or finds the oxygen and overlooks the hydrogen. We all know that any formula for water that doesn't include both hydrogen and oxygen doesn't . . . well . . . hold water. But this is exactly the kind of analysis we do when we practice selective editing. We see only pieces of the whole . . . only those pieces of information that lead us to a preconceived conclusion.

This is part of the process we spoke of before in talking about the Life Equation. When you have decided that the result will be negative, you accept as valid only data that brings about that negative conclusion.

Nell had been recently divorced and wanted to begin a new social life. But, she complained, it was all hopeless. "All the nice guys are either married or gay," she said. She had met one man who interested her—a resident physician at the hospital where she worked—but, she said, "he is not interested in me."

How did she know that? He had never asked her for a date. Wasn't that plain enough? "Does he talk to you at all?" Nell was asked. "Yes," she said. "We talk every morning. In fact, when I come to work, he usually has coffee waiting for me." "What do you talk about?" "All different things.

Sometimes he'll cut a cartoon out of the paper to show me. And we'll laugh about it."

Nell was willing to agree that this indicated that the young doctor liked her, but she insisted that if he liked her in a *romantic way,* he would have asked her out—and he hadn't. Nell disregarded all other evidence—conversations, coffee, and cartoons—because she was unsure of herself.

But one day Nell offered to buy her friend a cup of coffee in the cafeteria as a thank you for all the coffee he'd bought her. And while they were there, he jokingly said that he'd wanted to invite her to a hospital dance. "Why didn't you?" Nell asked. "Because you're married, of course," he said. "I'm not married," Nell said then. "I'm divorced. And I haven't worn a wedding ring since my ex and I separated. What made you think I am still married?"

"I asked one of the other nurses. She told me you were married," said the young man who supposedly "wasn't interested." "I guess she thought that because I didn't talk much about my divorce," said Nell. "Some people knew, but not everybody. . . ."

10. Disqualifying the Positive

This error of thinking is related to selective editing in that you draw a conclusion from only partial evidence, but it goes a step further. Those who disqualify the positive insist upon drawing conclusions only from that part of the evidence that is negative. That is, if twenty people tell you that "you look terrific today" and just one says that "you shouldn't wear green, it isn't becoming to you," which opinion (or opinions) do you count? Do you immediately feel terrific twenty times over, or do you feel green and ugly?

Unfortunately, it seems to be part of human nature to forget all the good things once a single bad thing comes along.

We tend to remember all the dumb things we did (and define our self-worth by them), while forgetting all our solid accomplishments. This is the "Yes, but" syndrome practiced on ourselves. "*Yes*, I did that well, *but* that's not the situation now." "*Yes*, that went right, *but* it didn't last." "*Yes*, that was wonderful, *but* it can never happen again. "It would have been great, *but* . . ." And, "*Yes*, he brings me coffee, *but* he couldn't be interested in me."

11. Mind Reading

Do we really think we can read other people's minds or that they can read ours? Can you guess what the person sitting next to you at the lunch counter is going to order before you hear what he says? If you can, you should get an agent and go on the stage.

Mind reading is another name for jumping to conclusions, as Julie (whom we met earlier in this chapter) did when she got that telephone call from Pete. A belief in mind reading can cause trouble in a variety of ways.

You might assume you know what someone else is thinking. ("There's no point in asking. I know what he'll say.") Then later you discover that you were wrong. And all you can do now is think, "If only I'd asked, this wouldn't have happened."

You may assume that you *should* know what someone is thinking. Jane's son committed suicide. She has convinced herself that this was her fault, because she should have known what he was thinking, she should have known what he planned. The notion that "a mother always knows" is one of our hardier myths.

You may assume that others in your life should have read your mind. "They should have known I was upset. They should have realized I wanted to be appointed to that job."

These assumptions are often a part of woulda/coulda/shoulda misery* You focus on what might have been if you had read another's mind correctly—or if another had read your mind correctly as you feel he (or she) should have been able to do. But the truth is that even though we sometimes make good guesses about what those close to us are thinking, and they about us, human beings do not have the power to read each other's minds. And we cause a great deal of misery when we act as if we do.

12. Personalization

This is the technique of taking as a personal affront an event that has nothing to do with you. This is the sort of thing that drivers do when caught in a traffic jam on the way to an appointment. "Get out of my way," they snarl (even though the other drivers can't hear). "Don't you realize I'm late?" No, of course, they don't realize. They're too busy grumping about the traffic jam themselves.

Nick worked out a reorganization plan for the sales department and sent it "upstairs" to the vice-president for approval. But the VP sent it back with a letter explaining that he has decided against reorganizing the department at this time. "He doesn't like me," concludes Nick. "He doesn't like anything I do. This plan should have been accepted, and it would have been if he had liked me." Yet it's possible that the VP either didn't like that specific plan or, for any number of reasons, has decided not to reorganize the sales force at the present time. Nick's conclusion that the VP's decision was "personal" may affect his relationship with that VP and put a psychological barrier in his path should he come up with another idea that the VP might want to see.

13. Fortune-Telling

This error of thinking assumes that you should always know what is coming before it gets here. Your internal crystal ball should have notified you in advance so that you would not make any stupid mistakes—such as marrying the wrong person or turning down a role in a play that later results in stardom for someone else.

A fortune-teller doesn't admit to himself or herself that it seemed like a perfectly good decision at the time, or even that it made complete sense, given the conditions that existed at the time, or that the person you married twenty years ago has changed. Or that you have. The fortune teller says only, "I should have known better," and then settles in for a long bout of self-recrimination.

There is a tendency in playing the what-might-have-been game to make an assumption that if things had gone in a different direction, the outcome would have been terrific . . . wonderful. The one who got away in love, like the fish who escaped the hook, grows bigger and better in memory. "If I had only married Larry," says Liz, "I'd be so happy today." Maybe so, but maybe not. Maybe Larry cheats on his wife.

If a time machine were invented, you might decide to return to, say, 1906, and do a good deed by giving the residents of San Francisco advance warning about the earthquake that would level their town in April of that year. You wouldn't be able to prevent the earthquake, of course, but, at least you could prevent loss of life.

Or could you? Would the residents of San Francisco heed your warning and leave town before the tremors began? Would they believe your story that you came from the future? Or might they not tell you, "You worry too much. There hasn't been a serious quake in California in a hundred years"?

It is certainly much easier to recognize a turning point in history or in someone's life than it is to know what would have happened had an event turned out differently. Sigmund Freud wanted to be a professor of neurology, but no university offered him that appointment. He turned instead to private psychiatric practice and developed psychoanalysis. If Freud had gotten the opportunity to do neurological research, would he have made some marvelous discovery about brain cells that has not yet been made? Would that mean that we would never have heard of psychoanalysis, or would someone else have had the same insights? Who can say?

When we let ourselves rewrite our own past, we tend to assume that all would have been well, if only . . . but we really don't know that at all.

14. The *Should* Syndrome

This is the belief that there is only one right way to do anything. And if you don't do it that way, you are a loser. You conjure up a set of expectations of how you think things should be—or what others say they should be—and then measure yourself, without mercy, against it.

When the bad guys in *Blazing Saddles* galloped up to the tollbooth, they were imprisoned in the *should* syndrome. All they could think was, "You should/must/have to/pay a nickel to get through the tollbooth, and since we don't have enough nickels, we are out of luck." They could not allow themselves to waive the rules—to mail in the coin later, to go around the booth—and thus make their way across the desert.

15. Emotional Reasoning

Once other errors of thinking begin to overwhelm your common sense, you are likely to find that this one follows almost automatically. You begin to *feel* inadequate . . . you begin to *feel* like a failure—and from this you conclude that you *are* inadequate, that you *are* a failure. Here again, your common sense may not be convinced of this, once you view the data objectively, but first you have to get your common sense into operation.

You may have been told not to think or use your common sense but rather to go with your "gut feelings." Using your common sense may have been called "rationalizing," "intellectualizing," or "avoiding the real problem." The belief that thoughts are somehow inferior to feelings is a theoretical view that is certainly not held by cognitive therapists. Because *how you feel* is affected by *how you think,* by how you perceive what is going on around you. You can let your thoughts get carried away by emotion or, by thinking more clearly, change the emotions you feel. By thinking more clearly, you can gain greater control over your own life and become happier.

WOULDA/COULDA/SHOULDA THINKING

All of the errors of thinking we have listed—and this is not an all-inclusive list—apply to woulda/coulda/shoulda thinking. However, they do not apply to everyone in the same way.

Some people are so overwhelmed by what has happened in the past that they see it as even more terrible than an objective outsider would see it. They heap blame and scorn upon themselves that they probably wouldn't feel for someone else. They see themselves then, as losers, as people who just don't "have it." This group can be helped by learning how to assess the past more fairly.

Some people are so disappointed by their present failure to

achieve expectations they had when they were young that they focus solely on what might have been and are unable to fairly assess what they *have* achieved—and what they could still achieve in the future. This group can be helped by learning how to assess the present and future possibilities more accurately.

Some people are quite realistic about what happened in the past, but feel so defeated by it that they are not at all realistic about the possibility of doing better or having more in the future. This group can be helped by learning how to assess future probabilities and possibilities less emotionally.

You may be among those who see the past as worse than it really was. You may be one who feels guiltier about what happened than is necessary. You may be relying too heavily on what happened in the past as an indicator of the future. Or you may be absolutely right about your disastrous past— and yet be quite wrong in the way you allow that past to block your future. Whatever is the truth in your situation, you can help yourself by learning how to analyze *exactly* what you are telling yourself. It is important to make sure that the conclusions you are drawing are not drawn from flawed or partial evidence.

WHAT BOTHERS YOU?

Now that you know a little bit about what we're going to do, let's get started doing it. Let's start by zeroing in on the memories you find so painful. Write down on a piece of paper the mistake, or mistakes, that continue to bother you. Write down those missed opportunities or injustices that continue to bother you. And write down all of the thoughts that come to mind when that mistake or missed opportunity or injustice comes to mind. Write down as many thoughts as you can, e.g.:

—"If only I'd taken that job offer in California."
—"If only I hadn't been so blind to what was going on here."
—"I'll never be able to advance in my career now."
—"I've lost the best chance I'll ever get."

Don't just come up with a list in your mind. Write these thoughts down. Seeing them in print will give you the opportunity to view them more objectively.

Now, make a list with three columns. In the first column list things that you should have done. In the second column list what you could have done about this at the time. And in the third column write down what would have been the consequences of that act . . . how do you think your life would be different today?

Should	Could	Result
Take Calif. job offer	quit present job	be making $50,000
Realized situation at office	been more aware of things	would have quit present job

Be specific. It's not sufficient to merely say, "I've goofed up my life." Or, "I'm a screw-up." (If you write that, you will immediately recognize that you are guilty of overgeneralization, won't you?)

It's important to stop and listen to yourself, to bring out the thoughts that run through your mind. You may never have put these thoughts into words before. You may say, I'm not thinking anything—I'm just unhappy. But you will find that you are thinking *something* when you are unhappy.

Instead of saying, "I should have done better," write down an example of a way in which you might have done better. Exactly what *should* you have done to produce this result? *Could* you have done it? Did you have the skills, money, experience, etc., at that time? If you had done it, what *would* be the result today?

Write down every wrong choice, every unfortunate event that you can think of. Write down what could have happened and then what would be the result in each case if you had handled the situation differently. Then gather your list or lists together and see if you can find the following errors of thinking in them:

1. All-or-Nothing Thinking

   ("If I can't have exactly what I want, I'll take nothing. If I'm not a complete success, I'm a total failure.")

2. Perfectionism

   ("I must do this perfectly, or I will be embarrassed. Or, I must be perfect, or no one can love me.")

3. Overgeneralization

   ("It didn't work once, it will never work.")

4. Global Labeling

   ("That didn't work out, which means nothing in my life will work out." "Everything I do turns out wrong. I'm a loser.")

5. Catastrophizing

   ("Something has gone wrong. That means disaster. The project is ruined. I'm finished.")

6. Minimizing

   ("I don't have enough talent to do the job." Or, "The

situation can't be as bad as everyone says. No need to
check.")

7. Comparative Thinking

   ("I don't measure up to others. Compared to them, I've
   failed.")

8. Uncritical Acceptance of Critics

   ("Others always know best. I can't trust my own judgment. If my girlfriend thinks this guy I like is a nerd, I
   better drop him.")

9. Selective Editing

   ("He can't possibly like me. . . ." Or, He can't think I
   am doing a good job, because he didn't invite me to the
   party . . ." or, "to the conference.")

10. Disqualifying the Positive

    ("Yes, but . . ." "Yes, that was wonderful, but . . .")

11. Mind Reading

    ("I know what he's thinking. There's no point in ask-
    ing.")

12. Personalization

    ("They didn't like my idea, therefore they don't like
    me.")

13. Fortune-Telling

("There is no point in trying. I know what will happen.")

14. *Should* Syndrome

("There is only *one* right way to do anything. You can't go through a tollbooth without paying.")

15. Emotional Reasoning

("I feel inadequate, therefore I must be inadequate.")

You may find it difficult to determine precisely which error of thinking applies to a specific thought. Don't worry. If you simply recognize that you are not being fair to yourself, whether you correctly distinguish all-or-nothing thinking from perfectionism is a minor point indeed.

It's possible, too, that you might feel confused because it seems to you that two or three categories apply at the same time. If you think that, you are probably right. As mentioned before, you'll find errors of thinking are rarely isolated, but seem to appear in pairs or triplets.

What is important, at the outset, is that you simply become aware that these errors of thinking exist and that you attempt to identify those errors that apply to you. Most of all, we want you to start the process of listening to the style and themes of your woulda/coulda/shoulda thoughts. Whenever you feel bad about the past, and about how decisions made in the past have short-circuited your future, make yourself aware of the exact thoughts that run through your mind. And check them for errors of thinking. (It may help you to look at the charts on pages 66–69. Both show how one woulda/coulda/shoulda thought can give rise to many errors of thinking. Chart 1 states the thought first, and then identifies the error of thinking. Chart 2 provides an example of the kind of thought described by each error of thinking.)

As you go through this book, you will become much more familiar with how these errors can creep into our thoughts about what we should have done, could have done, and what might have been done. You will also become familiar with how these errors of thinking affect what we think *can be done now*.

When you make yourself aware of your thoughts, you begin the process of getting through or going around your own personal "tollbooth." Admittedly, this probably won't make the tollbooth disappear. Whatever mistake, missed opportunity, or cause for regret exists in your life will still be a part of your past. But what *can* change is the way it is preventing you from moving forward.

Our goal is to help you gain the perspective that will enable you to find a way to reach the other side of the tollbooth rather than continuing to assume that the way is blocked or that there is no other side.

As you read this book, you will be able to move from the initial identification of your woulda/coulda/shoulda thoughts to dealing effectively with them. You will find that although you cannot change the past, you can, by changing your habits of thought, make it possible to change your future.

Chart 1

General thought:
   Mary says, "I should have married Joe. If I'd married Joe, I'd be happy today."

When Mary thinks:	She makes this error:
"He was the only one for me. No other man could ever replace him."	All-or-Nothing Thinking
"Since I didn't make the right decision, no other decision can make me happy."	Perfectionism
"I picked wrong once. I'm doomed to always pick wrong."	Overgeneralization
"I'm just a screw-up at relating or establishing relationships."	Global Labeling
"Not having married Joe, I'll always be miserable and lonely. I'll have no friends. Everybody will look down on me."	Catastrophizing
"The fact that Joe was a drug-abusing alcoholic criminal who was married six times before doesn't mean we couldn't have had a wonderful life together."	Minimizing
"All of my friends are married. I'll never have the happiness they have without Joe."	Comparative Thinking
"My mother keeps telling me that I've lost my only chance for happiness. She says I'm stupid for letting Joe get away."	Uncritical Acceptance of Critics
"The fact that I meet other men has no meaning. They can't possibly care about me, knowing how stupid I am."	Selective Editing

CHART 1   67

"If I'm as good as some people tell me I am, how come Joe rejected me?"	Disqualifying the Positive
"Joe should have known how much I cared for him without my having to tell him. I shouldn't have to say anything."	Mind Reading (Alternative I)
"I should have known what Joe needed from our relationship even though he never told me."	Mind Reading (Alternative II)
"The fact that I wasn't honest with Joe and he found out about Mel had nothing to do with his leaving. He just didn't like me."	Personalization
"I'll never be happy. I'll never have anyone."	Fortune-Telling
"I should have been more understanding. I shouldn't have thought of myself, only of him."	*Should* Syndrome
"I know I can never be happy. I just feel it. I just know."	Emotional Reasoning

Chart 2

General thought:
   John says, "If I had gone to law school, I could have been president of the company today instead of having this lousy, lower-level job."

This error of thinking:	Produces this thought:
All-or-Nothing Thinking	"There's only one way to success, and since I didn't choose it, I'll never be a success."
Perfectionism	"If I can't be president, nothing else can make me happy."
Overgeneralization	"Since I made the wrong decision once, I'm doomed to always make poor career choices."
Global Labeling	"I'm a loser."
Catastrophizing	"I'll always be an also-ran. I'll never succeed at anything. People will look down their noses at me."
Minimizing	"The fact that I wasn't interested in law school, or in law, and didn't have the money for tuition anyway, shouldn't have stopped me."
Comparative Thinking	"Everyone else in the world is successful. Everybody is more successful than I can ever be."
Uncritical Acceptance of Critics	"My wife keeps pointing out that I muffed my chance for success. She says I'm a loser for not going to law school."

CHART 2   69

Selective Editing	"The fact that I make a great deal of money at the job I now hold and have a private parking space doesn't mean anything."
Disqualifying the Positive	"Yes, I enjoy the work, but . . ."
Mind Reading	"I know what they think of me. Everybody thinks I'm a failure."
Personalization	"I know that when my colleagues talk about lawyers, they are really indirectly letting me know they think I'm a loser for not going to law school."
Fortune-telling	"I'll never be successful at any time in the future. Why? I don't know."
Should Syndrome	"I should have thought about my career when I was younger. I should have known I needed a law degree."
Emotional Reasoning	"I'm finished now. I feel it in my gut. I just know it."

Chapter Three

DO YOU REALLY WANT TO CHANGE?

Before we go into any further discussion about how you might change your life, we have to ask one very crucial question: Do you really want to? Do you really want to stop thinking about what happened in the past and what might have been?

Most people will say, "Of course I want to stop. I'm tired of thinking about what I've lost instead of what I can gain. I'm very unhappy. . . . Do you think I *like* being this way?"

No, you don't like being this way. And no, you don't like constantly reviewing your losses instead of making gains. But you may as well admit to yourself that you must be getting *something* out of doing so, or you wouldn't do it. That something you are getting out of your woulda/coulda/shoulda routine is what is keeping you stuck where you are.

Hard to believe? Maybe, but imagine yourself in this situation: You are feeling very thirsty, and there is a sink in the corner of the room. You go over to the sink and turn on the tap. No water comes out. You wait a minute or so. Maybe the plumbing is a little slow. Nothing. You fiddle a little with the faucets. Still nothing.

How long would you stand at that sink?

Once you realized it was dry . . . once you realized there would be no possibility of getting a drink from that source, you would look for some other way to slake your thirst.

You'd look for another sink, or a soda machine. And so it is with life in general. If you are getting absolutely nothing from a situation, you will leave it. However, the truth is that many situations in life are much more similar to poor plumbing than to a dry sink. That is to say, you find yourself at a sink that provides just enough water to keep you hanging around. A drip here, a drop there, a distant misleading gurgle or two. You can't quite slake your thirst, but you figure it's better than nothing, or maybe you tell yourself that this little trickle is all you are likely to find anywhere.

The hard truth is that even the most negative of situations can yield some satisfaction. Even wallowing in misery can have its advantages. It may enable you to hold on to a dream, to believe in a fantasy.

THE LURE OF FANTASY

Everyone indulges in fantasy to some extent. In the limitless realm of imagination we can see ourselves as softly romantic as the heroine of a Barbara Cartland novel or as invincible and indestructible as Rambo. We can daydream ourselves away from the humdrum and routine and into the more exciting life of a celebrity. We can daydream ourselves out of worries about paying the bills and into a life of wealth and ease.

Fantasy is an essential ingredient of sexual arousal. A sexy dream can cause an orgasm all by itself. Fantasy is the critical component of all creativity. Even the most practical of solutions may be born as a wild flight of fancy. Fantasy is a form of escape. Who among us has not drifted into daydreaming when trapped in a particularly boring situation? Prisoners of war who have been locked in mindless solitary confinement tell tales of saving their sanity by building an entire computer or putting together an automobile or furnishing a house all inside the walls of their imagination. Getting away from it all through mind-travel is a commonly used relaxation technique. You close your eyes and imagine yourself in a sylvan glade, or in a boat rocking gently on a lake, or lying on a sun-baked beach—any place you personally would find relaxing if you were really there.

Fantasy can be just plain fun. You buy a lottery ticket and imagine yourself winning $10 million. You revel in images of yourself living it up, even though you know that all you really have—and given the odds, all you are likely to get—is the paper the ticket is printed on. But so what? It's possible to enjoy fantasy simply as an expression of hope and optimism. It doesn't have to be a guaranteed promise of performance.

Imagination is a gift. It helps us deal with harsh reality. It enhances our pleasures—enabling us to anticipate the pleasures of a party before we even get there. It enables us to "cognitively rehearse" a performance or social encounter by visualizing it in advance. Many athletes do this—they mentally go through the moves they will have to make later, seeing the motion required to put the ball through the hoop, seeing each step in a skating routine, seeing the fly ball coming toward the glove . . . so that they can move with more confidence when the actual event occurs.

But for all fantasy's wonderful attributes, it can sometimes be a curse. This is the case when clinging to its modest pleasures means that you never make the effort to obtain the more substantial pleasure you really want that can be found only in the real world.

WHEN FANTASY IS HARMFUL

Fantasy is harmful—and a barrier to real accomplishment—when it becomes our *primary* way of relating to life.

Fantasy is harmful when it is self-deprecating—when, in imagining yourself doing things differently, you are only tormenting yourself for *not* having done things differently.

Fantasy is harmful when it becomes a substitute for life, rather than merely a pleasant diversion, as in the case of a man who, ten years after divorce, still spends half his waking hours conjuring up torments he would dearly love to inflict on his ex-wife. He may well get some sense of satisfaction from his imaginings, but he is also preventing himself from developing a new relationship that could provide greater and more enduring pleasure.

CLINGING TO SMALL COMFORTS

We may well recognize that our fantasies are not helping, and yet we don't want to let them go. Why not? Because they do provide a measure of comfort. It may not be much, but it's something.

Well, it *seems* like something, anyway. Fantasy can be amazingly realistic. When you leave Planet Earth for Planet Imagination, you feel you are still in the same place. Whatever you see inside your head you feel you can reach out and touch. And whatever you see inside your head may be much more appealing than anything you are seeing right now in the reality of your life.

We use fantasy to provide relief from anxiety or guilt. As long as you dwell upon the single route to happiness you did not take, you are excusing yourself from the effort of seeking out another route. By telling yourself that the past determines the future, you tell yourself that it isn't really your fault you are so unhappy today.

We use fantasy to provide a boost to a flagging sense of self. By telling yourself what you might have achieved, if only . . . you confer upon yourself a level of success you might otherwise never obtain. You certainly aren't going to obtain it by merely dreaming about it.

Lisa is a good example. Lisa tells herself, "If I had only gone to medical school as I wanted to, I'd be happy today." She can visualize herself as a physician with a stethoscope around her neck. And in this vision Lisa always sees herself as totally content.

It's a very flattering vision. It assumes that if Lisa had gone to medical school, she'd of course have succeeded in becoming a doctor. It assumes that if she had become a doctor, she'd enjoy it and do well at it. It assumes that if she had become a doctor, she'd be happy today.

All these assumptions might well be the case, even though not everybody who starts medical school stays through graduation, even though not everybody who becomes a doctor enjoys it or does well at it, and even though not everybody who becomes a doctor lives happily ever after. Some physicians are discontented at their status *within* their profession. But Lisa is never going to find out what might have been true for her, because fantasy is as far as she ever gets.

Hanging on to her fantasy about what her life would be like if she had become a doctor gives Lisa a sense of status she doesn't have in her day-to-day existence. She'd much prefer to see herself as what she "should have been" rather than as what she is, since the former is much more impressive. Sticking to fantasy enables Lisa to avoid the anxiety she'd have to face if she decided to actually take some action either to go to medical school today or come up with an alternative that even if not totally satisfying is at least better than what she has today. Lisa's fantasy doesn't make her happy, but at the moment it's all she has. And she doesn't want to give up what she has in order to seek more. She'd really like a full pitcher, but she'll settle for a drip.

A woulda/coulda/shoulda fantasy can also be a power trip. The mother who says her child would not have been injured if she'd been with him on the camping trip as she should have been may be feeling guilty, but she is also feeling powerful. She is saying that had she been along, she would have had the power to make everything go right. Maybe so, but probably not. You may say, "If only I'd told my father not to climb that mountain, he'd be alive today." That implies you had the power to give your father an order he would immediately obey. (That's a common childhood fantasy with little basis in reality.) "Don't do it, Dad," you say. And he immediately responds, "Your wish is my command."

In other words, moving past your woulda/coulda/shoulda regrets would require giving up the fantasy that you now have, or ever had, the power to alter events. To see the past more realistically means shrinking from an omnipotent God to a mere mortal. And not everybody is willing to do that. Some people prefer thinking of themselves as all-powerful even if this illusion makes them feel terribly guilty.

Woulda/coulda/shoulda thinking provides other comforting illusions. Among them:

The Illusion of Unlimited Skill

When you say, "I should have done something to save him or her from that fatal heart attack," you are implying that you could have—that you had the necessary skill and equipment at hand. Most often this, too, is a fantasy.

The Illusion of Unlimited Ability to Know the Future

When we berate ourselves for making a wrong choice, we may be angry that we did not act upon information that we obtained only after the fact. We like to believe that we could have seen into the future, if only we'd tried.

The Illusion of Unlimited Knowledge

Experienced commodity traders may decide to invest in grain futures because data on rainfall in Russia seems to indicate that the Russians will have to buy some of their grain supply from the United States. If you don't normally deal in commodities, you may not have recognized the significance of the lack of rain in Russia—or even known about it. But when you read that others have made a killing in the grain market, you think, "I should have invested in grain." You expect yourself to know all there is to know about everything.

The Illusion of Perfect Effect

This is the belief that you could obtain precisely the result you want today if you went back in history and changed a single detail. You might say, "If I had taken that job I was offered ten years ago, I'd be a partner of the firm today." This implies you would have been able to change only that *portion of history* that you have selected. But, of course, it's just as possible that if you had taken the job ten years ago, you might have been run over by a truck two weeks later. If one fact is changed, any fact could be changed.

The Illusion of Guaranteed Results

This is the fond belief that there will be no risks in this world. If you possess skills, knowledge, and power, you also possess a gilt-edged guarantee that everything will turn out as you wish. Many people admit that they are willing to take action as long as the results are guaranteed. Unfortunately, even the lifetime warranty on a luxury car only promises to fix problems for free—it doesn't guarantee there will never be a problem.

The Nostalgia Illusion

This is the haze that coats the past with a nice warm glow, like remembering childhood as a time of no worries. (Why then did we occasionally cry? Why did we want a night-light?) This illusion is in effect when we look back and say, "I should never have quit that wonderful job." Or, "I should have married good old Oscar." Looking back nostalgically, we see only the good things—not the ones that prompted us to (a) quit, or (b) turn Oscar down.

The Illusion of Unchanging Relationships

This is the belief that whatever relationship you had in the past—good or bad—would be exactly the same if resumed today. Anyone you envied then is still to be envied today. Or, if you got back together with your long-lost high school sweetheart, you'd be as happy now as you were then. Under this law, it is not possible for anyone to be affected by the passage of time, by experience, by anything.

There is no end to the variety of illusions that are possible. We can imagine anything we want. Fantasy allows us to feel we are more in control of our lives than it is possible to be—certainly more in control than it is possible to be with so little effort.

PROTECTING YOURSELF FROM YOUR HEART'S DESIRE

Woulda/coulda/shoulda fantasies are basically self-protective thinking. We protect our image of ourselves as powerful, brave, worthy of love, and successful (or at least having the potential for success).

Maria brags, "If I had turned in the paper I was working on, I would have gotten an 'A' in that course." But she did not turn the paper in, and as a result will fail the course instead. Maria doesn't want to fail—but she also does not want to turn in a paper that might receive less than an "A." She doesn't want to risk shaking her image of herself as an "A" student. She feels that getting anything less than an "A" would be humiliating—unless, of course, there is a convenient excuse. And so she simply makes up that convenient excuse. She says she didn't have enough time to write the paper. She says a book she needed for research was missing from the library. These excuses, she feels, protect her self-image as a person capable of excellent work—even if she doesn't actually do any work at all. By settling for this *illusion of success,* Maria gives up all possibility of achieving real success in the real world.

We all have a natural tendency to want to protect ourselves from any blows to our self-esteem, from any possibility of embarrassment. You have to have self-confidence straight from the planet Krypton (Superman's hometown) to care nothing at all about the image of yourself you carry in your heart and present to the world. We all know that when people talk about suffering "a fate worse than death," they mean humiliation.

Researchers at the University of Massachusetts once asked a group of sky divers if they became anxious before jumping out of an airplane into thin air. Yes, indeed, the sky divers replied, but not about whether their parachute would malfunction and not open. They worried about whether they might appear nervous in front of their fellow divers. They worried about whether they might goof up or freeze, and thus not merely die, but, worse, die ignominiously.

There is no doubt that it can be much easier simply to dream of the modern equivalent of a prince on a white horse coming to carry you away than to face the awful reality of blind dates, singles bars, and kissing a lot of frogs who may not turn out to be the prince. Thinking about what could be and would be if only dreams came true is undoubtedly the best protection in the world against falling for someone who does not return your affection. But that same protective barrier is also the best means in the world for eliminating the possibility of meeting someone with whom you would enjoy sharing your life. You have to ask yourself whether this is the level of protection you really want.

You may be protecting yourself out of getting your heart's desire. Living in a world of woulda/coulda/shoulda fantasy is a short-term solution that postpones a recognized need to find a long-term solution.

CALCULATING THE BENEFIT OF CHANGE

Maybe you have told yourself that you really do intend to take realistic, positive action—later. And maybe you have noticed that "later" has a way of becoming "never."

Are you being honest with yourself? The bottom line is whether all this woulda/coulda/shoulda thinking is getting you where you want to be.

You must ask yourself, "Just how *useful* is it to me to continue focusing on my regrets, my mistakes, my missed opportunities?" We'd be the first to agree that it probably provides a mild degree of mental balm. But besides that:

—Does it change anything?
—Does it convince others to do what you would like them to do?

—Is it motivating you to move in new directions?

—If you are pursuing a course of action to "get even" with someone who has wronged you, can you claim that person has even noticed what you are doing?

—Will thinking about the past enable you to actually travel back in time and get a second chance at the *exact same opportunity* now that you are smarter, braver, and have the advantage of hindsight?

—Will agonizing over "wasting the last ten years" of your life prevent you from wasting *the next ten?*

If your answer to any of these questions is no, you have to ask yourself why you continue. Does focusing on what might have been, what should have been, etc., make you feel better . . . or worse?

Here's another question: What is the *worst thing* that could happen to you if you decide to put the past out of your mind and change your approach to life?

Will you die? Will people on the street shun you? Will none of your friends ever speak to you again? If what is really going through your mind is that no matter what you try, you won't be happy, what have you lost by making some kind of effort? You aren't happy now.

In Chapter Two we talked about how the error of catastrophizing applies to thinking about the past—we assume that whatever has happened has imposed a life sentence of misery. And we arrange to give ourselves that life sentence by applying exactly the same kind of thinking to the possibility of change. You might say, "I'd like things to be different now—but there is nothing I can do because it will never work . . . and besides, *anything I try will make things worse.*"

Any change is scary, and when we are scared we use our power of fantasy to come up with scenarios of disaster. We imagine that a noise in the house was caused by a burglar instead of the cat, who usually causes noises. When nervous about change, we tend to see it as the equivalent of going over a cliff—with only two possibilities in store. You either fly or get crushed on the rocks below. We say, "I know I can't fly, so that means . . . oooooh."

In fact, the possibilities are rarely so dramatic. And as we'll discuss in a later chapter, there are ways to cut down the level of risk you have to take. In most cases, however, it usually turns out that the *worst* that can happen is that you end up right where you are now. That is to say, you don't get what you want. On the other hand, the best that can happen is that you improve your situation.

MAKING A DECISION

Breaking out of the woulda/coulda/shoulda trap means willingly facing some short-term anxiety in exchange for making long-run gains. It means losing, at least temporarily, the success you have gained in fantasy, in order to make an effort to achieve more than you have now in real life. It means deciding to give up the small comfort of fantasy to find the larger satisfaction you really want.

Being honest with yourself about whether you are willing to give up your woulda/coulda/shoulda dreaming means analyzing your feelings about changing. It means recognizing that just as we distort the way we consider the wrong turns our lives have taken—by assuming that making one mistake means all is lost, by assuming that what has happened once will always happen, by assuming that there is only one route to satisfaction—and that one is closed for good—we may also fall into the same negative patterns when we consider *whether* we can or should change.

We might, for example, combine the error of "fortune-telling" ("It will never work.") with that of "disqualifying the positive" ("Even if it works, it won't work well."). It comes out something like this: "Even if I could get started, I won't have the energy to continue. Even if I continue, I won't be successful. Even if I'm successful, it won't be enough. Even if it's enough for me, others won't recognize it. Even if others recognize it, it won't be the people I want . . . "and on and on and on.

Does any of that sound familiar?

It may be that when you hear a little voice inside saying, "Forget it, it will never work, nothing will ever change, it's too late . . ." this is not your voice speaking to you but someone else's. Have others actually said this to you? How accurately are you interpreting their views? How expert are these others? In making this pronouncement, are they really thinking of you—or of their own problems?

Remember that the uncritical acceptance of critics is another error of thinking. You have to ask yourself, "Who says?" People who refuse to forgive themselves for making a terrible mistake sometimes assume that others do not forgive them. But never ask. Never check. Never seek another opinion on whether there might be something more positive to do now than simply relive the past.

Of course, woulda/coulda/shoulda thinkers do not necessarily feel they need an opinion from anyone else. If asked how they know that "no change is possible," they will say, "I just know. Believe me. You just know these things, that's all."

That's not the kind of proof you would want to bet your house on. There is, of course, a law of *probability,* which says that given a certain set of facts, a particular result is likely a certain percentage of the time. But that is quite different from the all too common belief in certainty, which says that given a certain set of facts, the result will be whatever I later decide it would have been. Absolutely, positively, no doubt about it.

You can certainly increase the probability of a poor outcome if you insist upon setting a standard for "making a comeback" that is greater than anything you might have done, could have done, or should have done in the past.

Carrie made an error in a report she turned in to the head of her department. She was embarrassed when this was pointed out to her. Carrie determined that her next report would be error-free. But more than that, she felt that she could not now turn in "just any report." The next one would have to be so splendid, so incredibly wonderful, that it would erase all memory of her past lapse.

This can work two ways. Yes, determination to do better is a strong motivator for improved performance. On the other hand, a determination that you must do 200 percent better or there is no point in doing anything (perfectionism combined with all-or-nothing thinking) may lead to another cause for woulda/coulda/shoulda rumination. What will Carrie do if she realizes that the report she has prepared is good enough to turn in—but not incredibly wonderful? If she decides this paper, even if error-free, is still "not good enough" to turn in, she has set herself up for failure. She will do nothing.

When you do nothing, nothing happens. Nothing changes.

WHEN A DRIP IS ENOUGH

Some people will choose to do nothing. We have said that the goal of this book is to help those who want to give up their ruminations over the past and move on to a new way of thinking and acting. But we would be less than fair if we did not concede that some people will think that over and say no, thanks.

Some people want to maintain woulda/coulda/shoulda thinking because it gets their adrenaline flowing. It gets them excited. "Whenever I think of what I've lost, when I think of what I could have had if things had been different," says Jeremy, "my blood boils." He might not admit it, but Jeremy enjoys that angry sensation. Rightly or wrongly, he believes that no realistic level of accomplishment or happiness could equal the emotional rush he gets from simply reviewing the injustices, the indignities, the bad luck, the failures, the foolishness of his past. Jeremy would put this book back on the shelf unread.

Some people would prefer to stay Godlike even if that means a lifetime of suffering. If that's their choice, so be it. Iris feels that if only she had been home when her husband suffered a fatal heart attack, she could have saved him. She berates herself constantly for stopping to chat and returning home late. Yet she refuses to listen when a physician tells her that the damage was so severe, her husband could not have been saved even if he'd suffered the attack in a hospital emergency room. Iris wants to see herself as someone who could have made a difference . . . even if that means living with guilt.

Some people prefer the comfort of the known, even if it's miserable, to the risk of the unknown, even if it has the potential to improve their lives. Andrea knows her relationship with Stan is going nowhere. He makes it plain that he doesn't care about her—maybe he can't care about anybody but himself. Her friends don't know why she sticks with him. They ask, "Why don't you just break it off?" She doesn't because she is afraid that, miserable as she is with Stan, she will be even more miserable without him. She isn't willing to take the risk of being alone, even though that might open up the possibility of finding a new, more satisfying romance.

Some people refuse to let themselves off the hook. They have been taught—and deeply believe—that if you err, especially if you err seriously, then you should and must suffer forever. They believe that only continuous, unending suffering can redeem them from eternal damnation. They feel that, having erred, they do not have any right to happiness. Therefore, these people will do nothing that might make them happy.

Some people are totally convinced that the fantasy is the best they can get—and are not willing to debate the issue. Others would prefer a more realistic kind of satisfaction but are just too unassertive, too lazy, or too insecure. They lack the confidence to stick up for themselves. They won't ask to fill a job opening at the office, for example, for fear of being turned down. Instead, they hope that someone will nominate them for the post. They will say, "I'd rather stop suffering, but what can I do? I hope something happens to save me, but meanwhile I'll just sit here and be miserable."

GOING FOR MORE—AND BETTER

Some people say they want to change their lives, but all they do is sit around waiting for some *outside* event or person to come along and rescue them. If sitting around is all you are willing to do, then—to rephrase the greeting-card people— you don't care enough to want the very best.

If you merely think, "It would probably be a good thing to change," or if you are saying, "I won't get anywhere in my job if I don't change," or "I probably should change, because my spouse is really getting annoyed with me"—but you really don't want to make an effort and you aren't willing to take any risks, then you won't change.

Imagine a baseball game. The batter steps up to the plate. He holds the bat in position to swing. The pitcher hurls the ball. It connects with the bat. What happens next? It depends on whether the batter swings at the ball. If the ball merely hits the bat as the batter holds it in his hands, it will just bounce off. At best, it will become an easily caught blooper. Only if the batter puts the force of his swing behind the bat will the ball take off.

You could argue that even if the batter never attempts to swing, the pitcher might be so terrible that the batter would get a base on balls, and that this can happen in real life as well as in baseball. Very true. You can always wait and hope. On the other hand, you can decide to take a swing at it. If you want to come out swinging, read on.

CHALLENGING THE PAST

To move forward, you have to challenge the idea that what has happened in the past controls your future. You have to confront your thoughts about the past so that you can determine whether you are being fair to yourself.

Look again at the list you have made of wrong choices, regrets, and missed opportunities in your life. You have already begun to question whether the disappointment you feel has affected the way you view reality. You have checked your thoughts for errors of thinking. That is where you start becoming your own defense attorney—arguing your case before the jury of your mind.

Now, let us make that case even stronger. You can do that by applying the following specific techniques of analysis. These techniques are aids to clarifying your thinking—to bringing the power of your own common sense to bear on your situation.

Check for "Meaning."

Look over the negative words in your list and ask yourself exactly what meaning you apply to them. If you said, for example, "I failed at my job," do you mean you failed at one specific project? Or at everything connected with that job? If you said, "I was a jerk at that conference," exactly what did you do? Why is that episode so upsetting to you?

Meaning is a very individual thing. You may be upset and saddened by an event that most other people would welcome. That event may have a special meaning to you that it does not have for others. For example, a promotion is generally accepted as good news. But it is possible for an individual to be upset by a promotion if to him or her it means, "I'll have to move away from my friends, I'll be faced with challenges I'm not sure I can meet," etc.

The clearer you are about exactly what you mean—targeting the precise reasons you feel upset, and the precise thoughts that arise from that feeling, the better able you are to analyze those thoughts.

Recheck the evidence.

When you look at what you have written, you must ask:

—"What evidence do I have that this is true?"
—"Is this something I believe to be so, or do I have actual proof? Have I checked it out?"
—"Is the evidence reliable? How much faith can I put in the opinions of others?"

—"Is it emotional reasoning? Do I think, "It must be terrible," because I feel so terrible about it?"

Suppose you had written, "I married the wrong person. I could have married the right person. If I had, I'd be happy today." What is the evidence?

Did you marry the wrong person—at the time of the wedding? Or did this person turn out to be wrong at some later time? If this person was indeed wrong—and marrying him or her is a mistake to which you plead guilty, let us check the second part of the list. Was there a specific "right person" available to be wed? Or are you merely assuming that such a person would have shown up if you were not otherwise engaged? In other words, do you have hard evidence of this person's existence, or are you manufacturing evidence from an illusion? If there was a perfect person that you wrongly ignored, move on to the last part of the list. What evidence do you have that you would be happy today? Remember the Illusion of the Perfect Effect. Can you prove—beyond a reasonable doubt—that you would have lived happily ever after, that no inconvenient fact would have intervened? What is the source of your evidence? Is it credible? Question how you know what you claim you know. Do you just "think so"? You can think anything at all. Are you listening to what others "think," as opposed to what others can prove?

Check for bias against yourself.

Have you unreasonably "personalized" the situation or situations or your list? That is, many of us would say, "It was all my fault," even when other people wouldn't see it the same way. Many times people will say, "I know others wouldn't see it this way, but I do, because that's the way I am. I'm more responsible than others, so there is no excuse for me. I'm smarter than others, so there is no excuse for me."

The jury is listening. What are you going to tell them? Were there no extenuating circumstances at all?

Check for positives.

When you consider your present situation, the one in which what might have been has not happened, can you think of any advantage at all? Are you viewing the situation selectively—that is, seeing only the negative effects and omitting any positive ones? There is an old story about an optimistic child who is given a roomful of horse manure as a gift and is thrilled by it. Why? "Because," says the child, "with all this manure, there must be a pony here somewhere."

Even if you can't be all that optimistic about a load of manure, is there nothing good to be said? Have you met anyone you would not have met otherwise? Has any kindness been done that you would not have experienced otherwise? Is it possible this is a first step in seeing things in a new way?

Have you learned something from this adversity? It is often the case that your mistakes—as well as mistakes made by others—are valuable in teaching you what *not* to do.

Sharon was sure when she and Norman broke up that she would never get over him. But she did. She found that new friends, new interests, pushed memories of Norman out of her mind. Yet she still remembers the issue that soured their romance—his outrage when her work schedule interfered with plans they had made jointly. He accused her of caring more about her job than about him. Sharon felt guilty then. She felt she'd done something wrong. But now, looking back, she realizes that she needed a different kind of man. Knowing that has helped her find a new and better relationship with a man who admires her interest in her job.

Rick credits the success he has as a teacher today to his memories of teachers who bored and annoyed him as well as those from whom he learned a great deal. One teacher used to say, "That's a stupid question"—and so the students were afraid to ask another. Rick says that taught him to say, "That's an interesting question." And his students are encouraged to participate. He remembers a teacher who mumbled, so he makes sure he enunciates so that everyone can understand him.

It often happens that people can indeed think of a positive in their past—but they discount it. Someone will say to them, "You enjoyed the *early* years of your marriage." They will say, "Yes, but that doesn't count." Or, "You made some good friends at that job." "Yes, but so what?" Or, "You learned a great deal from that experience." "Yes, but it doesn't matter."

Such people will discount any positive in their own past behavior.

"You tried very hard."
"Yes, but that doesn't count."
"You meant well."
"That doesn't count."
"You didn't do it intentionally."
"That doesn't count."
"You didn't have all the information you needed at the time."
"That doesn't count. I should have."
"But you didn't realize it then. Everybody makes mistakes. You are only human."
"None of that counts."

Guilty. Guilty. Guilty. This is one tough client. But if you were the defense attorney for this tough client, you would list for the jury every fact that *any other* reasonable person would count as a plus. So you must do this for yourself. If you are fair to yourself, if you eliminate the negative distortions from the evidence you consider, you will give the jury in your mind the opportunity to unlock you from the past and give you another chance.

Check for value.

Always check the usefulness of your decision. The jury in your brain may be stubbornly unforgiving—still, you must ask yourself what value is derived from dwelling on the past. Are you getting anything out of it? Does anybody else benefit? Is it helping you to make a positive contribution to yourself or to others? (To give you an idea how to challenge your list of thoughts, look at the box on p. 92.)

In the next chapters, you will learn just why it is so difficult to get free of certain kinds of memories, and how to go about developing a plan for getting on with your life. There are chapters that specifically discuss how to handle a range of woulda/coulda/shoulda situations—such as how to handle feelings of revenge or how to deal with woulda/coulda/shoulda feelings that are stirred up by others.

By going forward to these chapters, you are proclaiming your desire to change your life—you are setting out to find a decent drink of water rather than settle for a drip.

Chart 3

Ann worries constantly that she is a bad parent. She had an unhappy childhood. She feels that if her parents had been more loving toward her, she would feel more confident as a parent now.

She thinks, "There is only one way to raise children, and since I wasn't raised that way, I can't be a good parent" (all-or-nothing thinking, overgeneralizing); "I'm sure my children will end up in jail or on the psychiatrist's couch" (catastrophizing); "Everyone else in the world is a better parent" (comparative thinking); "My children seem fine, but I know I'm letting them down" (minimizing).

Here are questions Ann can ask herself to challenge her negative thoughts:

Rechecking the Evidence:

Is there only one way to raise children? Is there any guarantee that if children are raised in a certain way, they will never have any problems? What evidence am I using to label myself a "bad parent"? Is there any contrary evidence? Am I looking carefully at all the available data, or am I looking at only part of the evidence? Is the evidence from a credible, reliable, objective, and honest source?

Checking for Meaning:

What does being a good parent mean? Whose meaning do I accept? Is being a good parent a single trait, or is it a collection of ways of behaving, relating, and feeling? Should everything I do be dictated by what happened to me as a child?

Checking for Bias Against Self:

Don't I have a right to stand up for myself? Being my own worst critic hurts me rather than helps me. It's reasonable to look at what I do with a

CHART 3   93

view toward improving, but constantly seeing myself only in the most negative ways only keeps me upset.

Checking for Value:

How does believing this help me? How does my constant thinking of my resentment against my parents help my children? Is it possible to be the kind of parent I want to be if I spend so much time rehashing my grievances?

Checking for Positives:

Isn't it possible that my unhappiness as a child has made me a more sensitive adult?

Chapter Four

MEMORIES OF THE FUTURE—
AND OTHER TRICKS MEMORY PLAYS

Why is it so difficult simply to forget what we'd like to forget? People who claim that "time heals all wounds" have obviously never suffered a woulda/coulda/shoulda dilemma. This is a wound that seems to defy time's legendary healing. Why is this so? Why, despite all resolutions to "put the past behind and go on," do certain memories continue to cause us pain?

It isn't as if our brains automatically remember *everything* they have been asked to register. Half the time, the very information you *want* to remember—like a phone number or a list you need right away, or the name of the restaurant you enjoyed on vacation last year—seems to be forgotten with the greatest of ease!

Alas, there isn't a single easy answer for why we remember some things and forget others. The process of memory is, to a large degree, still a mystery to be plumbed. But we do know a little about it. There has been a significant amount of research into memory, both from a neurological as well as psychological point of view.

THE NEUROLOGICAL VIEW

In recent years there has been an increasing amount of memory research aimed at understanding the relevant chemical reactions in the brain. Researchers hope to answer questions like: Why does brain injury sometimes lead to amnesia? Why do very old people—and sufferers from Alzheimer's disease—tend to lose short-term memory (e.g., they can't remember what they ate for breakfast) long before they lose their long-term memory (e.g., they can still remember things that happened fifty years ago)? And exactly how *does* the brain process memory information?

At one time experts believed that memory operated on a kind of one-cell, one-image plan. That is, a single cell in your brain would fire when you saw your grandmother. But recent research, notably that conducted by neuroscientists at the University of California at Los Angeles, indicates that a cluster of nerve cells in the brain must act together to learn and remember a face, a word, or any other information. This new research indicates that there isn't a single "grandmother cell" and another cell labeled "grandfather," but that the information is represented in the brain in a pattern involving many nerve cells.

Other research, at the Veterans Administration Medical Center and the Salk Institute in La Jolla, California, points to the existence of a chemical molecule called the "NMDA receptor" that seems to be a key component in the brain's memory circuits. It appears to be the monitor that allows calcium to flow into brain cells, strengthening the network of neuron connections that are said to constitute memory.

The point of this kind of research is that if we could understand exactly which cells in our brain remember what, and exactly what chemical process is involved in remembering and forgetting, then perhaps someday we might have the means to restore memory to those who have lost it, or to help the very old remember what they did yesterday as easily as they remember what happened during World War I. And, who knows? Someday there might also be a woulda/coulda/shoulda pill to deal with those events in our life that we remember only too well and would prefer to forget.

You could take this W/C/S pill first thing in the morning—and zap!—no more agonizing over the past, no more guilt, no more recriminations, no more anger. Like a cold tablet designed to alleviate cold symptoms without making you drowsy, the W/C/S pill could be formulated to enable us to remember just enough about the past so we don't make the same mistakes again, but not enough to ruin our day.

Unfortunately, we will have to wait a while—maybe forever—for that. Meanwhile, we can take comfort in the fact that psychological research can help us understand and deal with the woulda/coulda/shoulda phenomenon right now.

THE THREE LEVELS OF MEMORY

Psychological research asserts that there are three separate levels of memory to be considered: sensory memory, short-term memory, and long-term memory.

Sensory memory is fleeing memory—you ask the telephone operator for a number, get it, remember it, dial it. But the number is busy, and two minutes later you can't remember it to dial again.

Short-term memory involves remembering what you did yesterday, what you had for breakfast. It's the ability to hold activities, conversations, speeches, lists, and such in mind for a while. But just for a while.

It is short-term memory that seems to disappear when we are stressed. You are more likely to forget to pack something you want to take on vacation, for example, if you are anxious about missing the plane. Studies show that students do a better job of *remembering* material they have studied for a test when they have been told the test "won't count" toward their grade—and thus they aren't as uptight.

Long-term memory consists of those words and images that we keep around for the long term, as the name implies. These are the memories we put away, subject to recall whenever we need them. Long-term memory consists of information we have not merely learned but have *overlearned*.

These may be memories that have been reinforced through constant repetition. If, when you went to school, you said the Pledge of Allegiance to the Flag every morning, it's very likely that you can still remember every word of it—even if you have not said it for ten, twenty, or thirty years. This is so because you didn't just learn it, you relearned it and relearned it again. You practiced it so many times, it became indelibly engraved on your brain cells. It's quite possible that you still remember a telephone number you dialed frequently as a child even though it is completely useless information now.

However, long-term memory is usually memory that has meaning. You are unlikely to remember thirty words chosen at random for years, unless for some reason you said them over and over again. It's easier to remember a little ditty like "Thirty days have September, April, June, and November," than a collection of unrelated data. And more to the point, it's easier to remember an event that has affected your life than an event of only passing significance.

WOULDA/COULDA/SHOULDA MEMORIES

Woulda/Coulda/Shoulda memories are long-term memories that not only have meaning for us, but that we *also* practice quite often. When you continue to relearn a long-term memory, you not only keep it available for use but *always at the ready*. It's somewhat like the difference between the money you keep in the bank and the money you keep in your pocket. One you can get if you need it. The other you have with you right now.

Imagine, if you will, a couple who has been married a long time. They certainly can remember their wedding reception, since it had special meaning to both, even though they can't remember every single detail. However, when they look through their wedding photo album, they find those "forgotten" details come back to them. "Oh yes, I remember now. Aunt Millie wore a red dress." "Gosh, remember Uncle Elmer dancing with his shoes off?" All it takes is a reminder to get the recall process underway.

Now suppose this couple had made a habit of studying those same wedding photographs every week of every year of their marriage. What would be the case then?

The details would never get stored away. Through constant, repeated reminders, they would always be kept available for instant use. Uncle Elmer's shoeless dance becomes information as current and usable as whether they had coffee or tea for breakfast.

When you fall into a pattern of woulda/coulda/shoulda thinking, you are, in effect, reviewing an album in your mind, constantly refreshing memories stored away. Instead of packing the details away where you can retrieve them if needed, you are keeping them close at hand.

This practice is not always a problem. If reviewing that album brings back happy memories that cheer your day, that's fine. But if reviewing that album reinforces your unhappiness, you have to question why you do it.

RULES OF REMEMBERING

Dr. Gordon Bower, a Stanford University professor famed for his work in learning theory, offers a reasonable answer to that question. Dr. Bower's studies have shown that certain conditions are conducive to remembering—and this is true whether the memories are happy or sad, important or trivial, wanted or not, short-term or long-term.

He found that you remember best when the mood you are in matches the mood you were in when you learned or experienced the material or event you are remembering. That means that when you are feeling cheerful, you are most likely to remember events that happened when you felt cheerful. When you are in a romantic mood, you are most likely to recall other times when you felt equally romantic.

But of course this also means that when you are feeling blue, all those miserable events that cast you down return to haunt you. And those happier memories that might cheer you up don't come to mind.

Dr. Bower also found that people learn best material that matches their mood. In one study researchers read stories to depressed people. Some of the stories were upbeat, some were tragic. You probably won't be surprised to learn that the depressed people remembered the details of the depressing stories best. You've heard the expression "Misery loves company." When you are feeling bad about your own life, you are not usually in the best mood to concentrate on the details of somebody else's triumph.

Learning is also related to the *intensity* of our moods. The more powerful the mood, the better we remember. Thus, we tend to remember those times of our lives when we were happiest or most miserable. We remember the most exciting times. We remember the most embarrassing times. We remember the wonderful wedding. The traumatic divorce. Isn't it true that you remember the high points and low points of your life a lot better than its mundane, everyday events?

Finally, the interpretations you draw from your thoughts will also match your mood. That is, if you feel a particular way, you will think that way. If you are feeling depressed, you will likely jump to depressing conclusions like, "It will always be this way, it's too late, I'm no good and never will be," etc. And of course such negative conclusions only make you feel worse . . . which influences the way you think about solutions. When you are in a negative mood, it is likely that if a solution came right up and knocked on your door, you'd assume the noise was a wrecking crew determined to destroy the house.

Dr. Bower's studies explain why your friends are impatient when you don't immediately follow their advice to "just forget about it." Forgetting what happened seems quite a simple matter to them—because it *would* be simple for them. To forget about *your* problem, that is. It wouldn't be so easy if it were *their* problem.

You see, because they are feeling calm, they see things differently than you who are feeling agitated do. Because they are in a good mood, they can see positive possibilities and can't understand why you can't. Because they are in a good mood, they remember all the times they had problems that were solved—while you see only roadblocks on the path to solution.

MEMORIES OF THE FUTURE

We sometimes talk about how our memory "plays tricks" on us. Surely, memory is playing a trick on us when our pleasant memories insist upon going into hiding whenever we are in a bad mood. One particular trick played by memory that is a major source of suffering for woulda/coulda/shoulda thinkers is a phenomenon we call "Memories of the Future."

Here's an example of how it works: The man whom Susan had been seeing for three months suggested that they each start "dating others"—a gentle way of saying he wasn't ready to marry her then—and probably never would be. Susan was so devastated she considered "ending it all." At thirty, she'd had previous relationships that didn't work out, but never had she felt as depressed as she did now.

Why? Susan said it was because she was so sure that this most recent love was Mr. Right. She recalled how one day when they were looking in the windows of antique shops, she'd mentioned how much she loved four-poster beds. And he'd replied, "I love them, too." Pointing to a shop window, she had said, "Look at that antique quilt, it would be perfect on a four-poster." "You're right," he had said. They went driving on a back-country road one day and passed a stone colonial house with a FOR SALE sign on the lawn. "That's exactly the kind of house I've always wanted," said Susan. "Me, too," said Mr. Right. They seemed to agree on everything—even to the breed of dog they preferred.

Susan could see it all as if it had already happened. She could picture the two of them living with that dog in that house, sleeping in the four-poster bed covered by the antique quilt. In her mind's ear, she heard the conversations they would have there. Thus, when Mr. Right wanted to see others when he moved away from their relationship, he didn't merely leave her—he took her house, dog, bed, and quilt away with him. It was like coming home and finding that a bomb has not only wiped out the one you love, but destroyed your cherished possessions, too. In Susan's mind, she had owned those things. She had imagined that house so often, it became real. By constantly rehearsing her expectations, Susan had stored them in "memory" as if they had actually happened.

This is why the promotion that you don't get is not merely disappointing because you have been unfairly rejected. It is disappointing because you have been denied all the income, prestige, and opportunity you had anticipated, and perhaps *had already acquired in your mind.* When an unexpected hitch causes you to cancel your vacation plans, the sense of loss you feel is conditioned by the fact that you have "seen" yourself having a relaxed and wonderful time. If, instead, you had "seen" your cruise ship sinking in mid-ocean, you'd probably feel relieved to hear the trip was canceled.

MEMORY MENDING

Memory is such a tricky function that not only is it possible to "remember" things that haven't happened yet, it is also possible to rewrite the memories we have of events that have happened. Memory is not like a videotape recorder that captures images and then forever plays them back in exactly the same way. Memory can be revised. This is different from lying about what you remember. This means remembering a version of events that strays from reality.

Take Marty's story, for example:

On vacation some years ago, Marty was sitting alone in an outdoor café in Spain. A beautiful woman, also alone, sat down at the very next table. Marty tried to think of a great opening line to start a conversation between them. He wanted to invite her to sit at his table. He wanted to go out with her. Who knew what wondrous events might follow?

As he sought the right words, he worried, "What if she doesn't speak English? What if she is waiting for another man? What if she thinks I'm a masher?" By the time Marty got up enough nerve to actually say something, the object of his thoughts had finished her lunch and left. Marty never saw her again. But whenever he is reminded of his vacation in Spain, he inserts a new ending to the scene in the café. He pictures himself and the young woman together, laughing, going to her place.

This is not just a daydream he has now and then. He really does remember it that way.

And why not? It's certainly more enjoyable to remember being accepted than to recall being insecure. Marty has since developed the self-confidence to speak up to *señoritas,* so if he chooses to remember himself making out in Madrid, no harm is done. It's just a fond nonmemory, you might say.

But, unfortunately, renovating a memory is not always so harmless an occupation.

Dorothy is a case in point.

Dorothy feels overwhelmed by guilt because she sent her son on a community-sponsored bus trip that ended in an accident in which her son was killed. She feels guilty because her son didn't want to go on that trip, but she insisted. Now, she feels that he would be alive today if not for her. She forgets that at the time she insisted her son go on that trip, she felt she was acting in her son's best interest. She believed the educational experience would be "good for him." She forgets that she could not possibly have foreseen the accident. By adding the tragic knowledge that only came *after* the event to her memory of it, she now remembers doing something terrible that was not terrible when she did it.

THE ROSE-COLORED-GLASSES EFFECT

Sometimes we combine tricks of memory to create additional havoc. The rose-colored-glasses effect is a good example. First we improve an old memory, then keep it fresh by constant repetition, and then use it as the standard by which present circumstances are compared. It's not as complicated as it sounds. An example will make that clearer:

Adam's wife died when she was only twenty-four years old. They were just beginning their life together. When he thinks of her—and he thinks of her often—he sees her at twenty-four, not at forty-five, as he is now. She is still young and beautiful. When he thinks of their life together, he tends to remember it as one long honeymoon. He doesn't remember living through everyday annoyances such as the furnace breaking down or a quarrel over money or a dispute about the children, because these things never had a chance to develop. If there ever was anything about her that bothered him, he has long since modified his memory of it.

This might seem terribly romantic—if it weren't for the fact that Adam is a very lonely man. He wants to fall in love again—but he can't seem to meet a woman who measures up to the woman he lost. But how could any woman measure up to that standard? No real woman can be as perfect as a much-polished, idealized memory.

Anything that exists in the present will be seen to disadvantage if, when you assess it, you insist on taking off those magical spectacles you wear when reviewing your past. Thus, you can be married and dissatisfied with your mate because you compare him or her with "the one who got away," who is, of course, not only remembered as wonderful, but whose memory has been significantly improved by what you imagine has happened to him or her since. You can be dissatisfied with your present job because you remember the old job as much more satisfying than you thought it was when you held it. You are remembering the rewards while conveniently forgetting the drawbacks. Whenever you compare what you have to your modified, improved memory of what you had before, the present comes up short.

WHY "JUST FORGET IT" DOESN'T WORK

Advice to "just forget it" doesn't work because you can't simply touch a button on your head to turn off your brain. The kind of memory involved in painful recollections is not sensory memory, which falls away in seconds or short-term memory, which disappears in days. It is long-term memory—the kind that stays with us. It is memory that is reinforced by mood.

Therefore, although you may dearly wish you could "just forget it," it stands to reason that when you are anxious and unhappy you:

—will keenly feel that loss you have suffered (which then makes you feel even more anxious and unhappy)
—will be more receptive to arguments that support your negative feelings than to those that support a more upbeat attitude
—will tend to remember your failures more clearly than your successes
—will tend to *interpret all information in the most negative way*

WHAT DOES WORK

Keep in mind, however, that everything that is true about being in a bad mood (e.g., that it evokes negative memories and negative attitudes) is equally true about being in a good mood (it evokes positive thought and attitudes). Thus, it also stands to reason that if you can merely lighten the mood you are in, you will be:

—more likely to remember positive memories, as well as negative ones

—more likely to respond to positive suggestions and recognize positive data
—more likely to remember the times you were successful in addition to the times you were not
—a lot less likely to jump to the wretched conclusion that it's too late and all is lost

"Change your mood" may seem to be no better advice than "Just forget it," since there also is no "mood switch" attached to the human head. But experience shows that it is possible to change one's mood by changing one's thoughts. You can make yourself angry by recalling some incident that made you furious at the time it happened. You can make yourself feel more relaxed by deliberately conjuring up thoughts of activities you find enjoyable—like lying on a beach or strolling through a beautiful garden.

DIVERSIONARY TACTICS

These are diversionary tactics—that is, you divert one set of thoughts by substituting another. Diversionary tactics can be very effective in changing your mood and helping you to forget because they *interrupt* the constant repetition of those thoughts that put you in a bad mood in the first place.

Remember that the more you repeat something, the more likely you are to keep it in the front of your mind. When you continue to review a mistake, a missed opportunity, or a wrong done to you in the past, you keep the memory fresh, the injury current, the loss immediate, and the pain fresh. You also reinforce the bad mood—those low feelings—that naturally accompanied the original injury. In this mood, you are not likely to think clearly. You don't feel like planning for the future.

But if you can stop repeating those thoughts, you are more

likely to be able to forget them. Information that is not used tends to decay. Even if the information does not disappear out of long-term memory, at least it will move out of your mind's pocket and into the storage vault. Thus, to change your mood and thereby begin the process of forgetting, you must take some action that will interrupt your thoughts—even if only temporarily.

One handy technique—admittedly a minor one—for interrupting the constant repetition of an unwanted thought is called *thought-stopping*. It means consciously replacing one set of thoughts with another. Thought-stopping is a stopgap, a Band-Aid; but it can be helpful when you become aware that you are slipping into another woulda/coulda/shoulda rumination. Thought-stopping is like clearing your desk so that you can work on what is really important.

For example: The next time you find yourself saying, "If only . . ." start counting by thirteens from one to one hundred. One, thirteen, twenty-six . . . and thirteen more is thirty-nine, and thirteen more is . . . um . . . fifty-two . . . You will find that it is not only difficult to count by thirteens, but is practically impossible to do that and think about anything else at the same time. Thus, such counting can serve as a distraction.

Any diversionary tactic can be used to halt the automatic flow of woulda/coulda/shoulda thoughts. You can count backward from one hundred, sing along with a record album, clean your desk. A relaxation technique may work for you. A common one is to breathe in very deeply (so that your chest expands and your tummy rises a little). Hold your breath for five seconds. Then breathe out s-l-o-w-l-y, counting to ten. Repeat this twenty times. By concentrating on breathing, holding, exhaling, and counting how many times you have done each, you won't have much concentration left over for anything else.

Another breathing technique involves picturing a rectangle. The shorter ends measure 2"—or 2', it doesn't matter. The longer ends measure 4", or 4'.

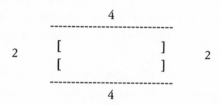

With this picture in your mind, you picture the top of the rectangle while slowly inhaling to the count of four. Hold your breath (and picture descending the side of the rectangle) for a slow count of two. Then exhale slowly, counting to four and picturing the bottom of the rectangle. Hold your breath again for a slow count of two, mentally ascending the fourth side of the rectangle.

Here's a thought-stopping technique that is amazingly simple—but most people refuse to use it. Get a rubber band, put it around your wrist. Whenever you have a tormenting thought ("If only . . ." "I should have . . ." "I mucked up . . ."), snap the band to give yourself a little sting. This is known as an aversive-conditioning technique. You literally teach yourself to avoid a thought that will (if you use the technique) result in pain. Why, you might ask, would I do something to hurt myself? Because you are hurting yourself more if you continue to dwell on what you can't change.

You aren't going to be snapping rubber bands or counting backward from one hundred endlessly. These are merely techniques to halt an unwanted flow of thoughts just long enough for you to turn your concentration to something else.

The *most important* diversionary tactic you know, however, is checking for errors of thinking. When you are upset, negative thoughts flow automatically through your mind. When you make yourself aware of those thoughts and analyze them

("Am I catastrophizing? Am I personalizing? Am I fortune-telling?"), you are acting to interrupt them. When you recognize the fact that you are exaggerating, jumping to negative conclusions, overgeneralizing, selectively editing so that all positive input is deleted, you act to change a defeated mood into a more positive, questioning, assertive one.

You realize now that if you start saying: "If only I'd married Joe"—other thoughts quickly follow. Like, "I messed up my life. I'll never find love now. No one could love me." And so forth. When you realize this is what you are thinking, you can say, "Wait a minute! I'm doing it again. I'm letting my thoughts run away. I can't be sure I've messed up my life—I don't know what life would have been like with Joe. I can't be sure that I'll never find love. . . ." etc.

Instead of allowing those negative thoughts to spin out of control, making you feel worse and worse—locking you ever more firmly into the past—confront them. Turn that internal monologue into a dialogue. Start asking yourself questions:

—"Is what I'm thinking really true?"
—"Am I making an instant judgment before I check out the facts?"
—"Am I turning myself down before anybody else gets a chance to do it?"
—"Is it really that bad? If it's that bad, is it hopeless? If I think it's hopeless, am I willing to ask another's opinion to see if others view my situation in the same way? Am I willing to check out at least some of my negative conclusions?"

When you question your internal negative thoughts, you interrupt their flow. When you interrupt that hostile bombardment, you will feel better. When you feel better, you are able to look at life in a more realistic way. And when you do that, you are ready to take the next step in turning your back on your past—and moving toward the future.

A CHANGE OF MEMORY

Achieving a more realistic outlook on life is a major accomplishment. But that alone may not bring about the degree of change you need. You may well be up against a pattern of thoughts so powerful that merely interrupting, questioning, stopping, or modifying them is not enough. They must be completely replaced!

How does one replace old memories with new ones? The most effective way to put old information into storage is to bombard the brain with *new information*. And you do that by developing a course of action that *forces you* to think about what you are going to do today and tomorrow, and thus takes your thoughts *away* from what happened yesterday. The brain can work on just so much at one time. If your brain is required to concentrate on new material, it simply will not be able to concentrate on that old material.

Even very depressed people, whose every instinct seems to cry out to stay in bed rather than get up to face another day, find that concentrating on a specific activity to be done lightens their mood. That activity can be something as simple as getting a cup of coffee or cleaning out the basement. The point is, when you force your mind to focus on a plan of action, that pushes other thoughts into the background.

The next chapter will discuss how to decide on a project that will help you, how to get started on it, and how to avoid the sense of futility that so often discourages efforts to bring about change. Your project might be one that is designed to fill a very specific lack in your life—like changing your job—or one that simply takes your mind off your own problems by helping others.

Marge, recently separated from her husband, said she still "hadn't gotten over" the shock of Hal's leaving. She thought of little else but their relationship, seeking to understand what had gone wrong. Sympathetic friends invited her to parties, but she didn't want to go. She didn't want to face the inevitable questions. She felt embarrassed, as if she were wearing a sign that read REJECT. She felt herself sinking into despondency. Then a neighbor asked her if she would volunteer at a local church's program for the homeless. "We need someone to help with the cooking," the neighbor said.

Marge agreed to volunteer. After work she went to the church. She not only helped with the cooking but found herself caught up in the problems of the homeless. She sought permanent apartments for homeless families. She made friends both with the others who were helping and with those being helped. Many times she was just too busy to think about Hal or herself. And one day she realized she really didn't want to think about Hal anymore. Her self-esteem had returned. Her interests had changed. She was ready to extend herself in other directions, to go to parties. She felt she had plenty of interesting things to talk about besides a marriage that was long over.

No matter what kind of change you make in your life, you may feel some mixed emotions about it. When you refurnish a room, you feel excited at the prospect of a new look. Yet at the same time, you may hate to see a favorite old chair go, broken and shabby though it may be. You may feel exactly the same way about "refurnishing" your memory. Breaking out of woulda/coulda/shoulda thinking may mean—in the short term, at any rate—giving up some fond memories along with those you wish you could forget. To stop thinking about the loss that accompanies the memory of a lost love, you may also have to stop thinking of the good times you used to have, of the satisfactions that the relationship brought you. It takes energy to turn from facing backward to facing forward—a lot of energy—and at the outset, you must do it without reservation. Cold turkey.

Essayist Charles Lamb wrote, "The good things in life are not to be had singly, but come to us with a mixture." The same is true of the bad things in life. Even a terrible marriage may have started well . . . may have had some wonderful moments . . . may have produced some wonderful children.

Even a career that careened into catastrophe may have had some triumphs. But if remembering the good in the past leads inevitably to woulda/coulda/shoulda ruminations about the bad parts, then all memory of that period will have to stop until the time comes when remembering doesn't lead to ruminating. If looking through old snapshots makes you sad, burn the photo album, and if you can't bring yourself to burn it, at least stash it someplace where you can't get at it until you feel you can handle it.

For the time being, you have to concentrate completely only on what you are going to do today and tomorrow. You have to concentrate on making some kind of change. You have to work at developing new activities that will result in "new memories."

When you have new memories, you will find that you have not totally forgotten what happened in your past or the people that were meaningful to you. However, you will have changed *the way* you remember. What is now the past that casts a shadow on your life will become the past that *used to* get in your way—but doesn't anymore.

Chapter Five

WHAT NEXT? MAKING CHANGE HAPPEN

Most people know what it would take to make them happy. They may think that what they want is unattainable— but they know what they long for.

Tina said, "I'd be happy if I could stop thinking about my ex-husband, but I can't." Asked what would have to happen to erase the memory of her ex from her mind, Tina replied, "I guess I'd have to fall in love again—but that will never happen. I wish it would happen—but it won't."

In other words, Tina is able to state a wish—but wishing is all she manages to do. And, unfortunately, wishing is not a very effective problem-solving technique.

No doubt you already know that wishing won't change your life. The fairy godmother with a wand is long overdue, so it is up to you to do something for yourself. And it is also up to you to decide precisely what that "something" will be.

- If you must pay for a past mistake, what is your payment plan? Do you intend to wallow in guilt or would it be better to come up with some way to make a positive contribution that will, at least in some measure, make amends?
- If you wish you had done something for your parents before they died, and obviously it is "too late now," is there something you can do now for the next generation?
- Even if it is true that you cannot get back what you have

lost or attain everything that you feel you deserve, can you at least think of something to do—just for starters—that will give you *more of what you want* than you have right now, or *move you closer* to a desired goal than you are right now?

More than likely, you have thought about a goal you would like to reach, an event you would like to see happen. You have probably wished for something very specific and yet done nothing to attain it.

Perhaps that is because you have said to yourself, "I shouldn't *have to* do anything. What happened wasn't my fault."

That is a very common reaction. If you feel you are an innocent victim or that you have already done more than your share to put things right, you may simply conclude that it is time that *somebody else* does something.

You may say, "I've put up with enough. Why should I have to do anything to clear up this mess?"

Or, "I shouldn't have to make the phone call. They should call me! They know I'm here. They know what I can do. It's time they showed me a little respect."

Or, "Look, if something is going to happen, then it is going to happen. I'm tired of trying to make it happen. Let fate take a hand for a change."

All of this translates into doing nothing at all to improve your situation. Because if you wait for others, they may do nothing. Those others may be fools. They may be lazy. They may be so caught up in their own problems, they don't even realize your problems exist. It may be reasonable to feel that someone else should step in and take action, but it is not a good idea to wait around for that to happen.

Another very common reason for failing to take action is a belief that "it won't make any difference anyway." You may say, "It's too late now," or "It won't work." Those two comments are usually followed by more generalized statements, like, "Nothing will work." "It's too late to do anything." "What's the use? There is no way to make a meaningful difference now."

All too often people who feel this way never ask themselves, "How do I know this is true?" Have you asked that question?

RECALCULATING YOUR LIFE EQUATION

"I know," you may say. "After all, this is me we're talking about. I know what I can do and what I can't. You say I'm wrong. But you don't really know me. Nobody knows my situation as well as I do."

Undoubtedly, you know your own situation better than any outsider could possibly know it. Yet you still might be assessing the data you know about yourself incorrectly. Remember the Life Equation described in Chapter One? It may be that you have already decided what the result will be before you actually added up the circumstances of your life. Thus, if you think of a possibility that might work, you immediately think "but it's too late" so that the conclusion will remain as gloomy as you previously decided it must be. "See there, I told you my situation is hopeless," you might say. "I knew it all the time."

You may claim you have reached your conclusion with scientific rigor. You have added up the disappointment, embarrassment, guilt, and/or loss you have suffered in the past and come to the conclusion that you are someone who has "lost the spark." Somebody who is "a goof-up." Somebody who is "too old." Somebody who is "weary of the fight." Somebody who "can't help it." When you look in the mirror, that's who you see. And you claim that you are not tinkering with the evidence.

The problem with that reasoning is the old familiar one of adding apples and oranges. Even if you are correct in adding up the result of what has happened in the past (keeping in mind that you may be distorting and taking too gloomy a view of it), that does not necessarily mean the *same conclusion will be the result of actions you take today as well as in the future.*

It can't be said too often: You cannot foretell the future. That's an error in thinking. You may say "I know," but unless you have a magical talent no other human possesses, you cannot "know." You can only theorize—and a theory requires checking. You cannot be sure something "won't work" until you have tried it—or until you have, at least, made a reasonable effort to determine the pros and cons.

You may well have received some very good advice before reading this book. You may have gotten some sound suggestions from friends. But, somehow, none of that advice "worked." Could that be because you had *already concluded* that it couldn't? ("It might work for others, but it will never work for me.")

For the time being, then, you must put aside your current Life Equation calculation. Shut it out of the house. Slam the door behind it. If you find yourself saying, "I can't ignore what I 'know' about me," then, for the time being, pretend to be somebody else. Pretend to be somebody who isn't carrying along the same baggage from the past that weighs you down.

Irving Berlin wrote that actors "may be broken-hearted but still go on." But non-actors do that, too. You don't have to be a performer to put a "brave face on" when you feel insecure, to look cheerful when you feel grumpy, to fake self-confidence when your knees are knocking. We are all required to be "actors" now and again. This may be one of those times. Even if you are sure that nothing will come of your efforts, pretend otherwise.

Acting the part of a self-confident and cheerful person can actually make you feel more self-confident and cheerful. Making an effort, even when you feel it is forced, can produce meaningful results. When we play a role, part of that role becomes a part of us. That happens because when we play a role, people react differently to us—and that changes how we feel. That change is not phony. It's real.

So pretend to be somebody who has just arrived from Mars. This person doesn't know how things are done here. This person doesn't understand the concept of "too late" or "not possible." This person (even though he or she "knows better deep down") is willing to try to do a little problem solving.

PROBLEM SOLVING

When you set out to solve a problem—any problem—you start with an open mind. That is, you assume, for the sake of argument, that somewhere, somehow, a solution exists. Some kind of solution. Finding that solution involves going through very specific activities. And these activities are the same whether you are attempting to resolve a woulda/coulda/shoulda problem or to develop a new medication that will cure the common cold.

You begin by searching for a specific goal or solution that you can work toward (without drawing any conclusions about what will work or what won't work or whether it is too late).

BRAINSTORMING SOLUTIONS

To search for a goal, start by attempting to think of at least a dozen or so possibilities. The greatest barrier to solving a

problem is not failing to come up with a solution; it is coming up with just one solution—and stopping there. That
isn't giving the problem a fair shot. It's something like going
into a restaurant and ordering a hamburger, only to be told
that you are in a vegetarian restaurant. "But I want a hamburger," you say. "Sorry," says the waiter. "We don't serve
hamburgers here. And this is the only restaurant open at this
hour of the night." What do you do? You can either look at
the menu to see if there is something else on it you can order
or go hungry.

Suppose you were studying a map to determine the best
way to drive from New York to Los Angeles. You could just
draw a straight line from one to the other and then attempt
to follow that route. But a better idea would be to study
several different routes. You could travel through Chicago, or
take a route that passes through St. Louis, or go farther south
to make a stop in Dallas. Your final choice might depend on
what you'd like to see along the way, or on the season of the
year, or on the actual distance of each route. The point is, the
more possibilities you can determine in advance, the better
your ability to find the route that will *suit you best.* That is
also true of finding the goal of a What-Next Action Plan.

Unfortunately, when we are in a woulda/coulda/shoulda
frame of mind, we tend to convince ourselves there is only *one*
right solution—a solution that is tied to the past:

—"If I hadn't broken up with John, I'd be fine."
—"If I were still the vice-president of the bank, I'd be fine."
—"If I had taken the job in Chicago, I'd be fine."
—"If I _____." (fill in the blank).

Such statements imply that if you can get back together with
John, resume the post of vice-president, or phone the people
in Chicago to say you've changed your mind, your problem is

solved. If you think that's the case, your course of action would seem pretty clear: Check it out. Phone John, the bank, or Chicago.

But what if merely changing your mind about a past decision and letting somebody know you've changed your mind doesn't do the job for you? You may be saying something that sounds more like, "If I hadn't driven my car that day, I wouldn't have been in that accident, and I'd be playing pro football today . . ."

In that case, you know that there is no possible way to cause an accident to "unhappen." There is no way to repeat several years of your life so you can do things differently. In that case, the solution tied to the past has passed.

That means brainstorming other solutions—solutions that do not depend on finding your way back to a path from which you have strayed, but which require finding a new path.

John is out. He has married someone else. What can you do? Wait and hope he gets divorced? Devote yourself more wholeheartedly to your career? Try to meet another man who might be even better for you? Sign up with the Peace Corps and have an adventure?

The bank is out. What can you do? Work for another bank, even if it means starting at a lower level and working upward again? Take your talents into another field? Run for political office?

If you can't play pro football, can you be involved in the sport in any other capacity? Can you coach? Can you become an expert on game statistics? Can you help get an amateur league going? Even pro football players eventually change careers. What other related career might possibly interest you? What other interests do you have?

When you brainstorm, no idea is too ridiculous to write down. There are many roads to Mecca, as the saying goes.

Don't rule out anything—even the most frivolous ideas contributed by your friends. You can be silly and serious at the same time, because you never know when the germ of a serious idea is contained in some truly off-the-wall suggestion. "Why don't I become the president of Ford Motor Company?" may seem to be a way-out question. But merely asking it could lead you to check out the possibility of getting a job at Ford. Lee Iacocca, once president of Ford and now president of Chrysler Corporation, started out as a local Ford salesman.

Don't discard an idea before you have had a chance to examine it. Don't refuse to list an idea because you "already know" it costs too much or would be too difficult. You can always cross out ideas later. It's easier to reduce a list of one hundred ideas to the best one or two than to try to come up with one or two choice ideas. Your goal is to move from the single choice that you woulda/coulda/shoulda made in the past to options that, even if they don't produce the effect you wanted, will still be better than what you have now.

THE REAL SECRET OF SUCCESS

The secret of successful brainstorming is to think in terms of "increasing the probabilities" rather than in terms of "guaranteed end result." If, for example, you feel, as Tina does, that only falling in love again will end your endless agonizing over the love you lost, you probably are not going to be able to come up with the name, address, and phone number of a new love. But you can brainstorm ways to meet new friends, who may introduce you to other people, who may invite you to a party where somebody special will be found. (And making new friends is likely to be more interesting than sitting at home bewailing a lost love in any case.)

If you feel you can "never" be as successful as you "should have been," brainstorm what you might to do to be *one step* more successful than you are now. Even a half-inch of forward progress is better than looking back.

Remember: Any activity that engages your attention, taps your energies, and takes up your time will push unwanted memories into storage.

Beware the automatic reaction—"It's impossible." You may say, "If that could work, I would already have done it!" But that is not necessarily the case. It often happens that what seems impossible becomes doable, if you follow up brainstorming by breaking up your ultimate goal into a series of intermediate steps and by keeping an open mind about whether all or any of these steps are possible until you have gathered all the information you need.

ONE STEP AT A TIME

Moving toward a chosen goal one step at a time is a major ingredient of success. Look over the list of goals that your brainstorming session has produced. Select one of them to check out. The checking-out process will enable you to decide whether or not you want to follow through and to discover whether your pessimistic views that it's too late or it won't work are correct. The checking-out process begins by breaking your ultimate goal into a series of intermediate goals.

Look at this way: If your goal were to reach the top of the Washington Monument, would you jump directly from the ground to the pinnacle, Superman style? Would you keep on trying to leap all 555 feet and 5⅛ inches in a single bound— or would you consider using the steps?

The steps, right? You would know instinctively that what

is impossible to achieve in a single jump is achieved quite easily once you decide to advance on it one step at a time. The steps would also be easier than attempting to walk up a plank tilted at a slope between the ground and the top floor. You can slip on a slope . . . but when you advance one step at a time, you can consolidate your gains before moving ahead again.

This is also true of making a desired change in your life. Change is too amorphous a concept to get a real hold on. If you focus only on the ultimate goal you wish to reach, it can seem so large and so far away as to be unattainable. Yet if you focus on the small steps that would be required to reach that goal, instead of focusing on that ultimate goal, you may find that the "unattainable" is within reach after all.

Consider this simple example. Suppose you were asked to make a list of the steps involved in making pasta for dinner. Could you come up with at least twenty separate steps? Number one is deciding to have pasta for dinner. Number twenty is serving it. Can you think of eighteen steps in between?

Perhaps you are saying, "C'mon, there aren't twenty steps involved in making pasta. There are maybe . . . six."

1. Decide to have pasta for dinner.
2. Heat pot of water to boiling.
3. Put pasta in water.
4. Cook required number of minutes.
5. Drain water.
6. Serve pasta.

Not true. There are many more. Where did the pasta come from? Was it sitting on the kitchen shelf, or did you have to go to a store to buy it? How will you measure the portion? Where will the pot come from? And the water?

Let's try that list again.

1. Decide to have pasta for dinner.
2. Look on kitchen shelf for pasta. The cupboard is bare.
3. Go to market.
4. Find pasta aisle.
5. Carry pasta to checkout counter.
6. Pay for pasta.
7. Carry it home.
8. Get pot out of cabinet.
9. Fill pot with water.
10. Put pot on burner on stove.
11. Light the burner.
12. Wait for water to come to boil.
13. Open package of pasta.
14. Measure quantity needed.
15. Put desired quantity of pasta in boiling water in pot.
16. Set timer for desired number of minutes.
17. Stir to keep pasta from sticking.
18. Obtain drainer from cabinet.
19. When timer rings, remove pot from burner.
20. Pour pasta and water through drainer so that water goes into sink and pasta remains.
21. Serve pasta.

That's *twenty-one* steps, and the pasta was only stirred once. And nothing was added to it. Coming up with a sauce for this pasta could take an additional twenty-one steps . . . or more.

Does this sound silly? It does only if you are an old hand at making pasta—only if you make it so often you don't even have to think about all the steps that are actually involved.

But look at this from the point of view of a young woman who has never made pasta before and who wants to make it now because her boyfriend loves it. She wants to do it "right." If she thinks only in terms of "Can I make a pasta dinner that will wow him?," she may conclude that she can't. "It probably won't be any good. He'll not only dislike my pasta, he'll decide he dislikes me." Etc. etc. etc.

However, if she decides to take on this pasta project *one step at a time,* she can *postpone the final decision* about whether or not she invites him for dinner. If she asks herself whether she can make a pasta dinner, she might answer no. But if she asks herself, "Can I go to a store?," the answer is likely to be yes. "Can I find the pasta aisle?" Yes. She might go to the store and buy a selection of prepared sauces—and make herself a pasta dinner every night for a week in order to decide which brand of pasta and which type of sauce she likes best. By taking it one step at a time, she gives herself the opportunity to gain the confidence required to make dinner for two.

This step-by-step rule applies to whatever goal you wish to reach, to whatever action you would like to take in order to change your life.

Therefore, once you have your goal in mind:

1. Make a list of the steps that would be required to accomplish what you have in mind.

2. Now rewrite that list adding at least 50 percent more steps. If you had four steps written down, make it six. If you had six, make it nine.

3. Rewrite the list again, looking for ways to break down the steps you have listed to smaller and smaller ones. Do you have to reach someone? Do you have to find out that person's name? Look up the number? Pick up the telephone? Dial the telephone? Ask for that person by name? Write it down.

Write down even the smallest, most inconsequential steps. There is no such thing as a step that is too small to write down. Because if you say, "Big deal, anybody can do that"— that's good. Because, in all likelihood, you will do it.

There is almost nothing that we do that cannot be broken down into steps. For example, two housewives who confessed that their hopeless housekeeping had endangered their marriages wrote a book on how they finally licked total slobdom. They wrote down every single task that might be required (dust table in hall, sweep living room carpet, wipe kitchen counter, etc.) on a separate 3″ × 5″ card. Then, each morning, they'd take a card and do whatever was written on it. They worked card by card by card. And lo, the houses that had defeated them were clean. Similarly, a writer who suffered total mental block at the prospect of writing an "entire book," solved the problem by deciding to write only a single chapter. And when that was done, she did another chapter. Then another. Until the book was finished. And only when the book was finished did she admit she'd written a whole book.

It seems that it isn't true that the shortest distance between two points is a straight line. The shortest distance between two points is a dotted line—one point after the other.

GATHERING THE INFORMATION YOU NEED

Just thinking about *what* you are going to do next is very important, because it encourages you to look to the future instead of the past. Making lists of steps enables you to think through how you will do it. But of course it very well may be that you *don't know all the steps that will be required.*

Therefore, it may be that the first steps you list are those involved in simply gathering information you will need to compile your next list. Gathering information is the vital link between *what* and *how*.

How, of course, is the matter that is so often ignored when friends offer helpful advice. "Why don't you become a network anchorman?" suggests a well-meaning buddy. Or, "Stop thinking about Don. Fall in love with somebody else." This is like saying, "I know how you can pay off all your bills. Just inherit a million dollars." It isn't that the advice is "wrong." You might agree that your sense of satisfaction and self-esteem would soar if you replaced Dan Rather tomorrow, fell in love again, or acquired even a fraction of a million dollars. But what you want to know is *how to go about it.*

That can require doing some research, asking questions. Get out your paper and pencil and write down what is standing in the way of your own pet solution. Lack of money? Lack of time? Lack of support from spouse or significant other? Lack of education? Your age? Each of these constitutes a separate research project.

A REMINDER: Remember, you have agreed that you are not going to automatically say, "It won't work," and "It's too late." Instead, you are going to ask:

—Is there some way it can work?
—*What would it take to make it work?*

For example, Patricia feels she is not getting ahead in her nursing career because she graduated from a two-year program rather than a four-year college. Every time she sees an R.N. with a college degree getting a position she feels she deserves, she sighs, "If only my ability were properly recognized, if only I had the same academic credentials."

Patricia can think of a solution to this problem without much difficulty: Go back to school and get the degree that could make a difference. But she can also think of reasons why that solution is "impossible": She can't take time off from work now. She has to make a living. She has family obligations. She may not have enough money to live on while she goes back to school. All of those reasons add up to "It's too late."

However, Patricia has promised that although she knows it would "take too much time and too much money," and that looking into going back to school will "just be a waste of time," she will check it out anyway.

She started by asking these questions:

—"How can I find out what courses are available, exactly how much they cost, and what time they require?"
—"Who might know something about this?"

Patricia asked those questions at work and got some suggestions: Ask the State Nurses Association; try the state accreditation agency; go to the local library and ask for information about nursing education; call a school that offers a nursing degree and see what that school requires. Ask whomever you talk to at that school about other schools. Check whether you can obtain course credit by taking an examination.

She followed up on all of these suggestions. And each time she explained her situation and her goal of getting a four-year degree, she was told of a school program that might be worth looking into or a person who might be worth calling for information.

Finally, she discovered that a small college within commuting distance of her home offered to give "life credit"— credit for learning in the workplace—in addition to academic credit. This school was willing to give her credit for her previous two years of study plus an additional year's credit for learning acquired on the job. That meant she could earn a

college degree in just one year. That made the goal approach-
able. Patricia proceeded to work out a budget. How much
would a single year of college cost? How much would
she need to live on? Could she work out an agreement to
work part time so that she would still have some money
coming in?

She discovered that it was not too late. She discovered a
plan that would work.

Before jumping to the conclusion that any plan will be
"too difficult" or is "impossible," gather information about
exactly what it will cost in terms of money, time, emotional
output, hard work, etc. Only then do you have a realistic
basis for coming to a conclusion.

CONSIDERING A "TRADE-OFF"

Life hands us very few easy choices. Would you rather be a
millionaire or a starving peasant? Are you going to say, "Let
me think that over?"

Real-life choices tend to be much more difficult. They
often involve giving something up in order to gain something else. In real life, a woman may decide to turn down a
marriage proposal from a man to whom she is attracted because, although he has many fine qualities, he does not like
children—and she has two from a previous marriage. She
would like the companionship he offers—but not at the price
he demands—giving up custody of her children to her former
husband.

In fact, the choice that you may have to make may not
only be more difficult than opting between wealth and pov-
erty, but also less clear-cut than choosing between gaining a
husband and losing your children. Sometimes, we are faced
with making a choice that involves multiple pros and cons.

When you consider a plan of action that will change your life in some desired way, you may find that it will also change your life in ways that you don't desire at all. At that point, it's a good idea to sit down, get out a pencil and paper, and put all the advantages and disadvantages of your proposed course of action in writing. It is possible, of course, to weigh pros and cons in your head, but that is not as reliable a method as making four separate lists.

No matter whether the choice that faces us involves going or staying, changing or remaining the same, trying this plan or that one, there are always four ways of looking at it. There are the advantages and disadvantages involved in doing it—*and* the advantages and disadvantages involved in *not* doing it.

You may think that a list of advantages and disadvantages of doing something would be simply a mirror image of the list of advantages and disadvantages of not doing it. But that's not so. It's true that the lists will be similar in many ways—but they will also be different in some ways. Thus, you will gain even more perspective on the choice you have to make.

The lists may differ even more if you are weighing the pros and cons of two separate plans of action. Let us say you have already made a decision to quit your job and seek another. You have been offered two positions. Your lists then would consist of the pros and cons of taking one job and the pros and cons of taking the other.

To weigh the pros and cons of your own plan:

1. Get out two sheets of paper. Draw a line down the middle of each. And at the top of each write ADVANTAGES on the left-hand side, and DISADVANTAGES on the right-hand side.
2. On page one, list the advantages and disadvantages of

pursuing a course of action that you feel has the potential to change your life for the better. On page two, list the advantages and disadvantages of pursuing that plan.

3. Put a number from zero to five next to each advantage and disadvantage on both lists—zero for "no effect," five for "very important."

Here's an example: Sam has lost his job. He has already spent a few hours being angry at his boss, a few hours feeling sorry for himself, a few hours feeling hopeless about his future, and *now*, it is time to get serious. It does not take him a few hours to decide what he should do next: He needs to get a new job.

But first he has to make some crucial decisions. He will look for a new job in the same city, but should he, at the same time, inquire at firms in other cities?

Sam sits down and draws up two lists. The first lists the pros and cons of confining his search to the same city, the second the pros and cons of the alternative—looking elsewhere in the country.

Confining the Search to the Same City

Advantages		*Disadvantages*
My ex-wife has custody of my son, and if I stay here I can continue to see him.	5	There is no comparable company in this city. I may not be able to find the same kind of job I had before. I may have to settle for a less interesting and/or lower paying position
I won't have the expense of moving.	1	
My friends are here.	3	

Looking Elsewhere in the Country

Advantages		Disadvantages	
I can probably locate a job as good as or even better than the one I lost.	4	I would not see my son every week as I do now.	5
I would find a new location exciting: new people, new scenery.	3	I would have to use up some of my savings to pay the costs of relocation.	1

Sam decided to stay even if it meant settling for a job that wouldn't make him happy. At first, he'd put down a five both for being in the same city with his son and for finding the right job. But on reflection, he lowered the job to a four. Once he had to choose between them, he realized that it was the job that went down in importance, not his son.

Sam might well have decided differently if his son had been older and thus more independent and able to travel on his own. He knows he probably won't be completely satisfied with his new job, but he has the satisfaction of having made an informed choice. He will be on the lookout for ways to improve his own situation, of course. He may move later. But for now he has opted for what matters most.

Sam will feel better about staying in the city because he has made a conscious choice—rather than merely "allowing life to happen." By exploring the pros and cons of his choice, he can see positive reasons for staying that make him feel better about doing that. Psychologists use the term "self-efficacy" to describe this process. And many studies show that "self-efficacy" makes people feel better about their lives.

Settling for less than your ultimate goal is not necessarily an unhappy experience. You might say to yourself: I'd like to have one million dollars. Yet, if someone offered you only ten thousand dollars, you might decide to accept it. You would most likely feel very good about having that money, even if you still don't have the million that is your ultimate goal.

RECHECKING YOUR CHOICE

When you analyze the lists of advantages and disadvantages you have drawn up, be sure to check them for distortions of thinking. After all, it's just as easy to jump to conclusions or think emotionally when you consider a *specific change* as it is to do that when you reject the very notion that change is possible.

For example, let us suppose that you have discovered a new job opportunity. In the list of advantages (reasons to take this job), you write: "If I say no to this opportunity, I may never get another."

Is that statement really true? What is your evidence? Do you just think so?

There are several ways that errors of thinking can distort your decision-making ability. When you consider your options:

- Do you insist that you come up with a "perfect" solution, i.e., one that will solve your every need? That's very difficult. Look at it this way: Even if the solution that seems possible is not perfect, will it at least move you *closer* to where you want to be rather than further away? If it isn't the finish, is it a start?
- Do you insist that if you "can't have what I should have by now," you'd rather have nothing? Possibly that is because you are only weighing the difference between "what I should have now" and "what I can attain" and not the difference between "what I can attain" and "what I have now."
- Are you catastrophizing—that is, imagining disaster that may not occur? You may think, "If I leave town, I will lose my son forever." But are you sure about that? What evi-

dence do you have that this is true? Does every divorced parent who leaves town lose all contact with children?

- Are you giving too much weight to advisers who are no more expert than you are? You may say, "My mother says there is no point in trying this. She says it's a terrible idea." Mother may know best—but she might not. How expert is your mother in this particular area? Have you asked anyone else?

- Are you being fair in allocating the positives and negatives in your plan? You may feel you don't have the ability to do something because you credit any accomplishment in your past to pure luck. Luck may be a piece of an accomplishment; it is rarely the whole.

- Are you overstating the effect of your past experience, as in, "I tried this once and it didn't work"? Do you assume nothing you do will work? You cannot know that.

TAKING RISKS

You may have found that even after you come up with an action you feel you should take—something that "might work"—you still don't do it. "I should call John," you say. Or, call the bank, or call Chicago. But you don't. Because you say to yourself, "What if he says (or they say) no? What if I repeat the same mistake I made before? I just can't face going through the same thing again. My pride won't let me."

Alas, all choice involves risk. No doubt that is why some of us do not like to make choices. When Mom asks, "Which flavor do you want, chocolate or vanilla," some people, rather than go through the hassle of making up their mind, will say, "Oh gosh, either one." All of us would like a guarantee that we will always do the "right" thing. We want to be sure that we will always succeed, that we will never be rejected or embarrassed, or lose money. But such guarantees are not widely available.

Sometimes you have to face the fact of risk. This is not necessarily a bad thing—even when the plan doesn't work. Author Ralph Keyes says he has talked to thousands of people about taking risks. He asks for a show of hands of people who took a risk that didn't work out. Many hands usually go up. Then he asks for a show of hands to determine how many people thought about taking a chance—but didn't. Then he asks how many in each group are sorry. He reports that those who risked and lost are much happier than those who thought about doing something—and didn't. The first group says, "At least we tried." The second group always wonders what might have been. The value of "no," you might say, is that, at least you "know."

When a patient told psychiatrist Alfred Adler he was afraid to take a risk, Adler is said to have replied, "Ach, you are such a coward now. You were so much braver as a child." The patient wanted to know how Adler knew what he was like as a child. Adler explained that all children are risk-takers. A child trying to learn how to walk bravely attempts a few steps, and usually falls down. But children don't give up. They may cry a bit. But then they try again. Adults, on the other hand, take this matter of falling down—both literally and figuratively—much more seriously.

That may be, of course, because adults are embarrassed by a stumble, whereas children are not. Yet we often think of our stumbles as more embarrassing than they really are. We think others are looking when they are not. We think others care when they do not. After all, they have stumbles of their own.

And the value of taking a risk—of risking rejection (asking for a date, applying for a job) or risking failure (attempting something new)—is that the answer may be yes . . . the result may be success. You can't win a contest unless you enter it.

REDUCING THE RISK LEVEL

You may find that you cannot avoid some degree of risk in the particular plan of action you choose. However, that doesn't mean you cannot reduce the risk level. That is precisely what you do when you advance on a goal step by step.

You may not be willing simply to quit your job and go off to seek another. But are you at least willing to get some information about whether opportunities exist elsewhere? Are you willing to weigh the advantages and disadvantages of the information you acquire? Are you willing to test the water by talking to someone in another organization or another field? Are you willing to at least inquire about whom you might talk to?

Although there is no guarantee that what you try will succeed, you can be very sure that if you do nothing, you will continue looking backward. You will continue thinking about all the woulda/coulda/shoulda choices you have no way of making now. By doing nothing, you protect yourself from risk—but, as we said earlier, you also protect yourself from breaking out of the past and getting on with your life.

By doing nothing, you allow those old memories to stay in the front of your mind. When you do something to change things, you are also pushing those memories into storage.

You may find it easier to take action if you ask yourself, "What is the worst that can happen?" Will you get shot for trying? Can you really not survive? Then ask yourself, "What is the best that can happen?" Isn't that worth taking a risk? Isn't it worth at least an inquiry . . . a small effort? Any-

thing that you decide to do is better than continuing to
ruminate unhappily about what you didn't do or did wrong
in the past.

TAKING ACTION

Remember the Chinese saying, "A journey of a thousand
miles begins with a single step." If you take a single step and
see how that works out, you are on your way, and who knows
how many miles you will travel?

Chapter Six

PLAN B—THE BACKUP PLAN

"I tried it, but it didn't work."

There is nothing more discouraging than a plan that doesn't work. There is nothing more demoralizing than to rev yourself up to change your life, overcoming all the doubt that past experience has instilled in you, pushing yourself to make a plan and carry it out—and then to have it bomb.

You thought that's what would happen, and now you have been proven right. What next?

—"That's it," you may say. "I was willing to go to school for a year if necessary, but now that I find out two years is required, that's too much. I quit."

—"I want to get into the field of work I think I should have gone into years ago, but I find I can't move into it at the same level I'm in now, so I can't do it."

—"I was willing to apologize to my mother, but she thinks I should apologize to my aunts, too, and that's too much, so I'll just stay alienated from my family."

—"I was willing to go out again, but it didn't work out. Men are too demanding. I'll just have to be lonely."

—"Yes, I did a better job on the second project than on the first, but it still didn't please the boss. If I take on another project and don't do it perfectly, I'll just feel humiliated, so I'm not going to try."

Psychologist Albert Ellis labels our tendency to try again
and then quit if the try fails as "stupid behavior on the part
of non-stupid people." Why is it stupid? Because the ultimate result is that you deny yourself what you want. If you
set a condition for success that says it must come on the first
try—or if you state you will take further action only if you
are guaranteed that, this time, success will come immediately—your condition may not be met.

It's certainly understandable that once you make an effort
that doesn't work, you may feel sorely tempted to turn this
new, unhappy experience into a justification for future inaction. Now, you have something else in your life to look back
on and say, "It might have worked if only I'd done it ten
years ago, or if only some other impossible condition were
met. The temptation is strong to simply give up. The temptation is strong to say, "I tried, what more do you want?"

The question is, What more do *you* want? And, How
much effort are you willing to put forth to get it? Are you
willing to take what you learned from your first effort and
apply that toward making your second effort even stronger?

Unfortunately, one of the things you learn from experience
is that even with the best will in the world, you may not get
what you want the first time. If Plan A doesn't work out, you
may have to come with a Plan B and C and D . . .

Most people don't want to hear this. Most people prefer to
believe that if you make the effort to overcome your past, you
deserve a happy ending. Indeed, that was the theme of the
movie *The Best of Times,* in which actor Robin Williams por-
trayed a man who could not get over the fact that twenty
years before, his high school team lost a crucial football game
because he didn't catch a pass. If only Taft High had beaten
Bakersfield, everything would be different. So he decides to
recreate the game to give himself a second chance. The plot
of the film centers on the difficulties he has persuading the

members of both teams—all adults who now have other interests—to reassemble on the playing field. This being a movie, the game-deciding play happens exactly the same way as it occurred before—and this time, of course, Williams makes the catch—and puts his past behind him.

In real life, of course, even if the game could be recreated so precisely, Williams might just as easily miss the catch the second time. After all, in real life even pro football stars are known to miss one or two—or more—passes in a row.

In real life the plot may not unfold according to our script—or even if it does, the result may not be as satisfying as we had hoped.

This is why, in real life, it helps to have backup plans. A backup plan can be as simple as trying the same thing again. The most successful salespeople are those who are willing to endure two hundred rejections before the first buyer signs on the dotted line. Some people marry their childhood sweetheart who was the girl or boy next door, but most people meet dozens, even hundreds, of prospects for romance before one pairing clicks. A backup plan can mean coming up with another plan, armed now with the knowledge gained from your first effort about what *doesn't* work.

Whatever you plan to do next, once again write it down step by step. Just because you have done this before doesn't mean you now can do it in your head. Plans become concrete when they are committed to writing. You can't get a loan from a bank for a business plan that you've "thought about" in your head. It has to be down in black and white.

We realize you may not want to even think about, much less write down, another plan. When you are feeling upset about a setback it's very easy to fall into the old familiar can't-be-done patterns. Like perfectionism: "It didn't work perfectly, so that means it wasn't worth doing at all." Like overgeneralization: "It didn't work once, so that means it will never work." And global-labeling: "That didn't work, which means nothing I do will ever work."

These thoughts wear you down more than any activity ever could. Isn't that so? When you are feeling discouraged, dismayed, distressed, you feel like a loser. You tend to notice (selectively) only those people who seem to have succeeded with the greatest of ease. The boy wonder who founds a multimillion-dollar computer company at age seventeen. The young woman who at twenty-nine is a contented wife, mother, partner in a major law firm, and is considering running for Congress.

But please also notice the rest of us. We're here, too. The ones who "keep on trucking" . . . the ones who get tired and discouraged but get up and try again. Because that's the only way to change anything.

THE ITSY-BITSY SPIDER OPERATING SYSTEM

There's a children's song—you probably learned it as a small child—called "The Itsy-bitsy Spider." The lyrics go something like this:

> The itsy-bitsy spider went up the water spout,
> Down came the rain and washed the spider out,
> Out came the sun and dried up all the rain,
> And the itsy-bitsy spider went up the spout again.

If you have made a few efforts at wrenching your mind from the past and getting on with life—only to come up against another obstacle—you may begin to feel like the itsy-bitsy spider. Every time you think you are going to make it up the water spout, you get washed away. At some point you conclude that there isn't much point in making the climb again, because it's bound to rain.

But think about this: Every time the sun comes out, another opportunity exists for the spider to try again. All that has to happen is for the rain to hold off . . . long enough . . . just once . . . and that bug is going to get where it wants to go. That's the real point of this song. That's why little children learn to sing it.

Of course, you might point out that it's easy enough for a bug not to take it personally when it gets washed away a few times, because insects operate on instinct. Spiders don't have to deal with all the pain humans suffer from rejection, failure, and embarrassment. That pain makes it harder for humans to brave the rain again and again.

Humans have to deal with the fact that although most people will *say* they admire someone who keeps on trying, they have a dismaying tendency to keep that admiration very well hidden until *after* the trying succeeds.

A political candidate who loses several elections in a row can count on being derided for "not knowing when to quit." And yet, if that candidate manages to win just once, public opinion turns around totally. Not only will a single success wipe out a history of defeat, but that very history of defeat turns the success into the stuff of legend. Overnight "that fool who doesn't know when to quit" becomes "the gutsy go-getter who refused to quit"—who "ignored the naysayers," who "had faith in himself or herself when no one else did," who "stuck it out and won."

Most of us, of course, are not attempting to achieve public acclaim; we merely want to move ahead in our lives—to make amends for an injustice, to advance a stalled career, to find a new love, to regain acceptance from friends and family. And we ask, "How many efforts does *that* take?"

We'd like to say "only one." But experience dictates that

we have to say, "It might be only one, but it could be many."

That doesn't seem fair. "I tried," you may say. "It took a lot of effort for me to do what I did. I spent money/time/emotion. I took a big risk. And now you are telling me it isn't enough. That I have to go through this again. I shouldn't have to. It hurts. And I don't want to get hurt again."

We're back to the same problem you faced when contemplating Plan A—that if you protect yourself from hurt by not taking an action, by not taking any risk, you may be protecting yourself from getting your heart's desire, from the possibility that, in the end, you will change your life.

If the only alternative is continuing woulda/coulda/shoulda thinking, how attractive is that? Is it really better than making another effort to climb the spout?

TRYING AGAIN

In making the effort to try the same plan again, it helps to expect the best instead of the worst. When you assume in advance that your efforts will be futile, you are more likely to *hear a negative reply* no matter what is said. Take, for example, the story of Tom, who asks Alice for a date and is turned down. She says she can't go out with him because she has to study.

Before Tom had asked Alice, he'd said to himself, "She probably won't be interested in me." Thus, when Alice says she has to study, Tom thinks, "She says she has to study, but I know that's just an excuse. What she *really* means is that she doesn't like me. So, there is no point in calling again. She will never go out with me."

If, on the other hand, Tom had "assumed the best"—that

is, if, when he approached Alice, he'd thought that her answer might be yes—he would be much more likely to accept her statement at face value. That is, she has said she has to study because that is the truth. Thus, if Tom asks her again, she will be happy to go out with him. The only way to check it out is to ask Alice again.

Obviously, the next question is: But what if Tom was right the first time? What if Alice really *was* making up an excuse rather than admit she isn't interested? What if Tom asks again and is turned down again?

The answer is that when Tom thinks of possible reasons for that refusal (as he quite naturally would do), he must, once again, assume the "best" instead of the "worst."

The "worst" would be that Alice is the elected representative of all females everywhere, and that, since she has decreed it, no other woman in the world will ever go out with Tom. Therefore, there is no point in his even trying to meet anyone else.

But, surely (assuming the "best"), it is possible that Alice has simply made a mistake in rejecting the opportunity to get to know Tom better. Everyone makes mistakes. It's possible that Alice is secretly pining for another. She doesn't want to go out with anyone else. Or it's possible that Alice is simply a person whose needs just do not mesh with Tom's. None of these reasons reflect badly on Tom—or on his potential to meet another woman who would find him attractive. In other words, just because Plan A (a date with Alice) didn't work out, there's no reason not to start initiating Plan B (a date with someone else) right away.

And what is true about Tom's effort to improve his social life is true about the kind of effort—and thought process—required to meet any goal. What is true about trying again to get a date with Alice might be true of trying again to get anything. If one college turns you down, are there other colleges? If one employer says no, are there other employers? If your first suggestion is rebuffed, does that prove no suggestion will ever be welcomed?

MODIFYING THE PLAN

Of course, trying again does not necessarily mean doing the same thing *the same way,* even if that were possible. As we've said before, we *do* learn from experience. If you touch a finger to a flame, the pain will teach you not to handle fire in the same way again. We modify our behavior to enhance our strengths and overcome our weaknesses. It is usually the case that the pitch the sales representative makes improves considerably between the first rejection and that 201st approach that finally succeeds. The itsy-bitsy spider may, by trial and error, discover the best time of day or season of the year for the spout to remain dry.

You may discover from your first effort that you need a skill you don't have. That could mean modifying your plan by reading up on a particular subject or taking a course or getting some training. Instead of saying to yourself, "I made a fool of myself making that presentation, I'll never attempt to make a presentation again," you say, "I need more skill and confidence. I'll take a course in public speaking so that when I make my next presentation, it will go well."

DEVELOPING AN ALTERNATIVE

It could be that after realistically assessing your situation, you recognize that taking the same route again—even if modified—is not the answer for you. Sometimes there really is a thing that can't be done.

If that's the case, Plan B then has to mean trying something else, maybe something totally new.

Best-selling novelist Jeffrey Archer tells a story of striking out in a new direction when, at age thirty-four, his career took an unexpected plunge. Until that time, Archer had experienced one success after another. He had been elected to the British Parliament and was widely viewed as having a brilliant political career ahead of him. That opinion changed abruptly after it was revealed that he'd borrowed heavily to invest in a company that turned out to be a fraud. Publicly embarrassed and facing financial ruin, he resigned his seat in Parliament and sought employment in private industry. His initial plan was to contact the many people he knew in high-level positions who could help him obtain a post. But that plan didn't work. He discovered that the businessmen and bankers he called on didn't want to offer a top-level job to someone whose investment decisions had not only been wrong but extensively written about in the newspapers. But they also did not want to offer a lesser—and less visible job—to someone with his background and qualifications.

Archer confronted the need for Plan B. He sat down and listed his strengths—among them the fact that he was a good storyteller. That led him to fantasize about telling the story of what happened to him. And that led to imagining a story of how somebody who has been cheated in business gets revenge on the crooks who bilked him. Archer turned all that imagining into a novel that became the first of many successes.

Obviously, not every Plan B will have such excellent results, but you never know, and there is always Plan C . . .

Novelist F. Scott Fitzgerald's line that "there are no second acts in American lives" is much quoted, but if it were ever true, it is an outdated idea now. Today, American lives are less like one-act plays and more like continuing daytime serials. We write the next chapter of our lives by focusing on What Next, by coming up with Plan B.

CHALLENGING THE ASSUMPTIONS THAT DISCOURAGE YOU

If you find yourself unwilling to come up with Plan B, it's time to do a reality check.

Why have you decided that further action is hopeless?

Is it because you demand that:

1. *The change you seek must happen quickly and easily—or not at all?*

   Have you considered whether it is better to spend the next five years making efforts to have a better life, so that five years from now you may be happier than you are now—or whether it is better to spend those five years bemoaning the better life that you don't have and still won't have at the end of them.

   Are you deciding on a plan that requires a minimum of effort but also offers only a minimum possibility of success?

2. *The result must be so marvelous that no one in the world can doubt that, at last, you are vindicated or absolved.*

   Are you setting up a Plan B so impossible that you are setting yourself up for defeat? That is, are you more determined to prove that you are right in saying it's hopeless than to prove you can do better?

   If you are determined that the only way you can face the world on terms that will make you happy is to become a television anchor—when you have no experience at any level in TV—you are not serious about changing. If Plan A was to become an anchor and it didn't work out, maybe Plan B should be getting a job in TV, or determining what educational level the television industry requires of its employees—and getting the required education.

3. *Do you demand that any plan you undertake be totally without risk?*
   Whenever you say, "What next?," you accept risk. There is risk in doing anything, but there is also risk in doing nothing. Is it better to say, "I really gave it a good fight," or to say, "I would have tried if I'd known for sure it would have worked"?

4. *Do you take the failure of Plan A as proof positive that you are worthless? Have you tried to come up with other possible reasons for that failure?*
   The college of your choice turns you down, the date of your choice says no, the editor of the magazine returns your article with a printed slip that says "no, thanks"—is this conclusive proof that you are unwanted, or—as we mentioned earlier—merely an indication that you need a Plan B college, date, or editor?

5. *Do you assume that Plan B must be a close variant of Plan A?*
   Just as you brainstormed for Plan A, think as broadly as possible about Plan B. Fantasize. Leave nothing off your list. Cross out later. The second act of your life does not have to be from the same show as the first. Mario Cuomo tried to play pro baseball for the Pittsburgh Pirates, but he didn't make it. He swapped sports for politics and, Plan B, became governor of New York.

6. *Do you assume that Plan B will be harder than Plan A, and Plan C harder than Plan B, and you feel your energy level is too low?*
   There is no way to predict whether the next step will be

harder or easier—but it certainly isn't guaranteed to be harder. It may well be easier simply because you become more adept at planning, more aware of what can go wrong, and because each step you take moves you further forward than you were before. If you fall, you don't fall as far.

It could be, for example, that you decide to go to college to get the degree you need to pursue a particular career, but after you get the degree, there are no job openings in that field. That's the bad news. But the good news is that you have a college degree, and that changes your game plan, increases your options, opens up new possibilities that were not there before.

THE SATISFACTIONS OF NOT GIVING UP

"When I didn't get invited to my high school prom," says Ann, "my mother said, 'Someday you will laugh at this.' She was wrong. I never laughed. But I found out that in the end, it didn't make any difference. Much worse has happened to me and I've survived. That knowledge helps me cope with what comes next."

There is pride to be taken in not giving up, in returning to the fight. People look with respect on those of whom it is said, "He (or she) is not a quitter."

This time when you focus on what next, do an analysis of the difficulties of Plan A. What didn't work? At what point did you get stuck? Take that step and break it into two or three smaller steps. This may make the step possible to climb now, or it may take you in a new direction.

What matters most is that you *stay active,* that you stay focused on your goals for the future. As you move forward, you will discover destinations you never thought about before. You can then decide where, among these destinations, you would like to go.

Chapter Seven

GRABBING HOLD OF YOUR LIFE

It would be nice if there was a single, easy-to-remember sentence that would sum up everything we'd like you to remember from this book—something on the order of "What's done is done," or "Don't cry over spilt milk." But sayings like that have been around for generations—and widely ignored for the same period of time.

They are ignored because even though we know such sentiments to be just common sense, we also know that when we feel overwrought, common sense is, quite literally, the furthest thing from our mind. When we are agitated, angry, or distressed, we jump to negative conclusions, see only the negative side of the story, assume that the worst has happened or is about to. This is no way to deal with reality.

Therefore, what we hope you will take away from these pages is not a simple phrase or magical incantation but a *process*—a process for grabbing hold of your life. We cannot emphasize too strongly that the techniques of cognitive therapy constitute *lifetime tools* to be used now—and continuously into the future—to combat that terrible feeling of being trapped in the consequences of past choices, past injustice, or past bad luck.

We mention the possibility of using cognitive-therapy techniques in the future, because even when you are successful in packing your woulda/coulda/shoulda thoughts away, they may not stay away. From time to time, you may come up against a reminder of your past that will unlock those thoughts again. And just as a successful dieter does not necessarily lose all desire for chocolate cake, a reformed woulda/coulda/shoulda thinker is likely to find that the *temptation* to give in to hopelessness and/or inertia may recur—and have to be fought off again. And again. But, fortunately, unlike the chocolate problem, the task of digging oneself out of a woulda/coulda/shoulda thinking rut gets easier and easier with each success.

The final chapters of this book will describe and discuss ways to deal with some very specific woulda/coulda/shoulda dilemmas. But before going on to them, let us pause now for a review of the cognitive-therapy process—in definitely more than a single sentence.

This review is repetitive by design because—as the memory experts tell us—we remember best that which we reinforce through repetition. But in addition to reinforcing the steps of cognitive therapy in your mind, this review will also include some warnings about those tendencies that have the most potential to undermine your efforts. ("Forewarned is forearmed"—to quote another common-sense saying.)

THE COGNITIVE-THERAPY PROCESS

1. *Make yourself aware of precisely what you are thinking when you feel "tied up in knots" about what has gone before.*
   As we pointed out before, woulda/coulda/shoulda thinking is so automatic it becomes a habit—like locking the front door or driving a car. A practiced driver can start the car while talking about something else. But if asked to become aware of the thoughts involved in starting a car, a driver can describe the process step by step. In a

similar manner, you can surface the thoughts that automatically run through your mind when you think about
the past. You may seem to be thinking only, "I feel like
dirt," when, in fact, you are thinking a great deal more.

2. *Write those thoughts down so that you can read them, so that
   you can study the exact words you are using.*
   Sometimes just putting down your thoughts in black and
   white is enough to get your common-sense motor going.
   People often look at what they have written and say, "Oh
   c'mon, that's ridiculous."

3. *Analyze your thoughts for the errors of thinking described in
   Chapter Two.*
   You don't have to pinpoint precisely which error applies,
   since as often as not two or three will apply at the same
   time. However, if you become familiar with the errors of
   thinking, you will easily recognize their presence in your
   thoughts. (In another section of this chapter we will provide questions you can put to yourself in this analysis
   process.)
      Eventually, you will get to the point where you will
   instantly recognize when your thoughts are falling into a
   woulda/coulda/shoulda pattern ("Uh-oh, here come those
   old negative thoughts again"), and you will be able to
   assert your common sense to calm yourself down and
   chase the debilitating thoughts away. You'll be able to
   interrupt your internal monologue and turn it into a dialogue.

4. *Brainstorm goals for the future.*
   If you could change your life, what changes would you
   like to make? Name one change that would make your

present life better in some way. What would you like to have? What would you like to do?

5. *Break the problem down to workable parts.*
What would be required for you to reach this goal? What would you have to do? What help would you need from others? What resources are necessary? Write down as many steps as you can think of . . . and then break those steps down into smaller ones. You may start by gathering information, writing down the steps you can take to obtain information. Whom do you ask? Where do you look?
Remember:

- Think in terms of increasing your chances, of broadening your opportunity—rather than in terms of final result. If the goal is to get married, you increase your chances by widening your circle of friends, finding places where potential friends are likely to be. If it involves getting a new job, you increase your chances by taking steps to determine what opportunities exist, by investigating where you might look.

- Think in terms of moving closer, not of "being there." Think in terms of improving your situation, even if you can't "have it all."

- Think in terms of reducing the risk by taking one small step at a time.

6. *Analyze possible alternative courses of action by making separate lists of the advantages and disadvantages of pursuing—and also not pursuing—each one.*
Ask yourself what trade-offs you are willing to accept, what constraints must be accommodated.

7. *Prepare a backup plan (Plan B) going through the same steps as required for the first plan.*

If we had unlimited skill and knowledge, every action we took would be the right one. But we are not perfect. Sometimes we have bad information. And when that happens, we make bad choices. At that point you don't have to quit; you can either try again or try something else.

If you feel you have been living life on the itsy-bitsy spider plan (move forward, experience setback, move forward, experience setback), you have learned that there can be setbacks—but you know, too, that you can recover and move forward again. You also know that experience is never wasted if you learn something from it. You may recall that an expert is defined as someone who knows all the mistakes that can be made, having already made them.

8. *Take action.*

Don't just stand there. Do something.

THOUGHT ANALYSIS

Remember that as you go through each step of the process, you must be aware of what you are thinking so that you can catch distortions of common sense before they trip you up.

Watch out for all-or-nothing thinking. This, surely, is one of the major barriers to banishing woulda/coulda/shoulda misery.

—"If I can't have what I should have had by now, I'll settle for complaining about it."
—"If I can't undo what I did in the past, I won't do anything at all."

—"If I want steak but it seems that all I'll be able to get for my efforts is hamburger, I'll just continue eating swill."

When you feel all-or-nothing thoughts taking over, *you* must take over. You must remind yourself again that even if the past is "the pits," you can improve the present and the future. You must remind yourself again that sometimes starting with hamburger *leads* to steak . . . while sticking with swill will not necessarily make it taste better.

Remember that the most troublesome words in the world are *everything, nothing, always, never,* and *should.* These words must not be allowed to discourage you from moving forward.

I've never done anything right.

Never? Not one correct action in an entire lifetime? You have never been kind . . . ever? Never written a check that didn't bounce? Never driven a car without an accident? Never cooked a meal that didn't burn? Never?

Nothing can be done.

Nothing? Or are you really saying that you cannot have the one choice you would prefer? Do you mean nothing can change the past—or do you mean nothing can change the future? Even if it is not possible to do something big, might it not still be possible to do something small that will make you *feel* better?

I should have done it differently.

It might have been better. What use is it to focus on what you should have done then as opposed to what you can do now? Can you prove it would have been better? If you can, can you change it?

Here are some more "thought warnings."

1. *Beware the might-have-been trap.*
Remember that the heart of the novelist beats within us all. We can all make up stories of "what might have been if only." How do you know? Can you prove it? Can you prove that had you gone down another road, you wouldn't have gone over a cliff?

2. *Beware the demand for one-step, guaranteed, perfect, and immediate results.*
Are you thinking you can't change the future because whatever you think you might do now "won't be good enough, fast enough, sure enough," etc.? Do you have "enough" right now? Even if the result of doing something still won't be "enough," might it not at least be a step up, a step forward?

3. *Refuse to permit your past to determine your future.*
Do you insist that what happened once is now the rule that will apply forever? That bad luck in one area of your life means you are "unlucky" in everything? Try to think more like a baseball player. In baseball, a .400 batting average is the mark of a megastar. But .400 means that the player succeeded in getting a hit only four out of ten times at bat. A ballplayer doesn't give up after a few strikeouts. Are you benching yourself before anyone else has a chance to do it? Usually, there is more than one way to play the game. If you can't hit, maybe you can pitch—or coach.

4. *Refuse to allow a setback to trigger those old feelings that "this is the end of the world."*

Ask yourself:

Has whatever disaster I believe will befall me actually *happened yet?*

What is the probability that it will, in fact, happen? What proof do I have?

MORE QUESTIONS

Questions, of course, are the core of cognitive reasoning. Only when you question what you are thinking can you detect the exaggerations, distortions, and unproved conclusions that keep you locked into the mistakes and missed opportunities of the past. Ask yourself:

—"Am I denying myself opportunity by doing nothing?"

—"What information did I have available at the time I made the decision?"

—"In regretting that decision, am I now adding information I did not have then?"

—"Am I seeing only the negatives? What possible positives am I overlooking?"

—"When making comparisons, am I comparing all the facts about myself and others?"

—"Do I know all the facts about the others?"

—"Am I comparing now with the past instead of now with a possible future?"

—"How do I know my conclusion is correct? Am I just assuming it?"

—"Do I really know what others are thinking or doing?"

—"How valid is the advice I have been given by others?"

—"Is this other person an expert? Is there someone else I can ask to double-check?"

—"Is there another possible explanation for others' behavior? Is their behavior changed, or do I just think it is because I'm in a bad mood? What are they like to others? What were they like to me before?"

—"If I don't know an answer, can I find it? Whom can I ask?"

TAKING ACTION

Remember that the way to cause bad memories to fade is to replace them with good memories, and the way to do that is to do something—to move ahead, to get involved in a project, to investigate possibilities.

Remember, too:

It is important in planning your future that you be fair to yourself. Do not set a goal so high that you can't possibly make it. But, also, do not accept a goal for yourself that is so low it amounts to an acceptance that nothing can change. Either way would be setting yourself up for a new round of woulda/coulda/shoulda.

Your plan for yourself must be reasonable. If you tell yourself that your past strikeouts can be forgotten only if you bat a thousand from here on in, that's impossible. You can never win.

At the same time . . . remember the Life Equation. If you accept the idea that whatever you do *must* end badly, you will act to bring about that result. By not asking for another's help, not calling to ask about a possible opportunity, or not issuing a second invitation, you turn yourself down before anyone else gets a chance to do it. The worst that can happen is that you will be turned down—but the best that can happen is that you will be accepted.

Some people will do nothing unless they feel that their effort is so perfect it guarantees success. If they believe their effort has even the *slightest chance* of being unsuccessful, they simply give up—and thus lose *any* chance of being successful. Some people won't make an effort to succeed because they have decided, in advance, that failure is guaranteed. Natalie admitted that she'd become careless about the quality of the résumés she sent out. She was using a copying machine that smudged the copies. "What's the difference?" she said. "They don't read them anyway." Natalie had arranged a self-fulfilling prophecy. She made herself unappealing to prospective employers, either because she had come to believe she wasn't worthy of being hired, or because she wanted an excuse (a poor-quality résumé) for not being hired that would be easier to bear than personal failure.

There is a middle course that can avoid a lifetime of woulda/coulda/shoulda. You do the best you can even if it's not perfect. You try to move your life forward even if it's not as far as "what might have been."

A rival at work got the job you believe you deserved. You may say to yourself, "I should have been more aggressive. I should have played the political game." Or, "This isn't fair. The boss should have given the position to me." But merely thinking about where you went wrong or the wrong done you does nothing to change the situation. If you focus instead on what you can do next, you might think of ways to improve your standing with the boss in the future; or you might decide to challenge the decision by filing a suit; or you might look for an alternative path to career advancement—such as becoming active in the professional organization that represents your field or looking for a new job. You might decide to seek satisfaction denied you at the office by becoming more involved in social or civic activities that have nothing to do with your work.

Whatever you decide will be a second choice. You may feel that whatever you decide will not fulfill you as much as that much-coveted job (although you cannot know for sure whether this will be so, since you can't foretell the future). But a second choice is usually better than nothing. Everything is relative. Would you rather watch TV or clean the house? Would you rather clean the house or take a test? Would you rather take a test or have a migraine headache? Would you rather have what you have now—or something *better?*

THE CONSEQUENCES OF MAKING A CHOICE

Let us reemphasize the point that making any choice involves consequences.

Your choice may involve risk.

Risk means stress. Stress creates anxiety. If you protect yourself against all anxiety, you may also protect yourself out of the goal you hope to achieve. The choice is not between total acceptance or dying . . . there is usually a course to be found somewhere between laid-back and laid out.

Your choice may require cutting your losses.

A woulda/coulda/shoulda thinker will say, "If I admit that I've been wrong to stay angry and vengeful about my divorce, I'd have to admit that I've wasted the last ten years of my life. I can't do that." But can you go on wasting ten more years of your life? Do you want to say, "How do I get that guy?" Or, "The heck with that guy. I'm getting on with my life." Ask yourself, "What's in it for me?"

We've all heard wonderful stories about somebody who twenty-five years after inventing something is finally given the credit and compensation that were unfairly denied him at the time. It's always nice to see someone vindicated. It's great when a wrong is finally made right. But the most interesting question is, what happened to that person in the twenty-five years in between? Some people get satisfaction out of seeking justice—the quest alone is enough. But others stay miserable until justice is obtained. And what if the wrong is never made right? You have to make the choice that is best for you.

The alcoholic says, "I should never have started drinking." That's true, but so what? The question is, "Do you plan to go on drinking or stop?"

Your choice may involve compromise.

You may not be able to get what you want unless you leave the town in which you live—and maybe you don't want to do that. You can't have both. Which will give you more of what you want? Is there something you can do to make your choice better, even if it will never be perfect? If you can only improve one facet of your life, isn't that worth doing? Some people insist on stamping their feet and saying over and over, "But I want it, I want it, I want it." As any three-year-old can tell you, that rarely has the desired effect.

Jennifer and William, both deeply religious Roman Catholics, were close friends for ten years and wanted to marry. But William was legally bound to a wife from whom he had separated after a brief and disastrous marriage. He had applied for a church annulment, and while they waited, Jennifer and William lived apart and remained chaste. The annulment finally came through and they were free to wed, but a week before the wedding date, William had a heart attack and died.

Jennifer's friends made no secret of the fact that they felt she had been cheated by waiting so long to live with William. Jennifer questioned herself. But when she reviewed the reasons why she and William had lived apart, she realized they did what was best for them at the time. If they had defied their church, guilt might well have driven them apart in a matter of months—and then they wouldn't have had the long and close friendship that both enjoyed.

It might have been better if William had not married hastily when he was very young. It would have been better if the annulment had come through earlier. It might have been better if William had had annual medical checkups. If, if, if . . . If frogs had wings, they would fly.

Your choice may involve simply coming to terms with the fact that even though your past mistake was every bit as disastrous as you say, the only thing you have the power to change is your future.

HELPFUL SUPPORT

When you make the choice to move ahead in your life—and you are ready to brainstorm ideas, to gather data, to make a plan—you may find it all much easier to do if you have a support system in place. Sometimes the suggestions of others help prime your own idea-pump. Others may be more optimistic about your options than you are.

But, a word of caution: Your family and friends may be your best support system—or they may not be. Your family and friends may only reinforce woulda/coulda/shoulda thinking. (This problem is discussed more fully in Chapter Thirteen.) You may already know this to be the case, or you may find out once you start discussing your ideas.

Try, then, to stick to discussing your plans with friends who are supportive or even neutral, rather than discouraging. Constructive criticism is fine. If someone says, "I don't think you are asking the right people," that may lead you to find others to ask. But if somebody says, "There is no way to do that," get a second opinion.

This is a nation of support groups—of people with singular problems getting together to support each other's efforts to change or adapt—groups like Alcoholics Anonymous, Gambler's Anonymous, or Parents Without Partners and such. There is no Woulda/Coulda/Shoulda Anonymous that we know about, but you may be able to start your own by forming a partnership with a friend who also wants to make a new start. You might check with a cognitive-therapy center near you to see if there is a group meeting there that could be of help to you.

But as helpful as the support of others may be, your own decision to change remains the key ingredient for success. You begin the process of change when you challenge your negative woulda/coulda/shoulda thoughts about what happened then and set your sights—and your thoughts—on what you will do now.

PART 2

*Conquering the Common
Disablers*

Chapter Eight:

THE TERRIBLE *SHOULDS*—
COMING TO TERMS WITH
YOUR PERSONAL STANDARDS

John Greenleaf Whittier put it this way: "For of all sad words of tongue or pen,/The saddest are these: It might have been!'"

Not quite right. The saddest, by far, are these: *It should have been. Should* is a word with so much potential for misery-making that psychiatrist Karen Horney has written of the "tyranny of Should" and psychologist Albert Ellis recommends banishing *should* from our language.

When we use the word *should,* we are usually putting ourselves down: "I should have known." "I should have found the money somehow." "I should have been wiser or kinder." "I should be thinner (or richer or whatever else) today." "But I wasn't and I'm not, so what else can I conclude except that I am a total failure, a loser, and a worthless husk?"

Admittedly, not every mention of *should* is equally troublesome. If you say, "I should leave this job because there isn't any challenge in it for me anymore," you are merely opening up the possibility of changing jobs. But on the other hand, if you say, "I should have left this job long ago," you are no longer talking about problem solving in the future, but of feeling guilty about the past.

The remorse we feel about things that we did—or didn't do—in the past can be such a powerful force that people will cut themselves off from any happiness because they feel they "don't deserve it." Some will even kill themselves because they feel they "do not deserve" to live.

You may feel that it is overstating the case to blame a mere word for stirring up such tidal waves of emotion, but *should* is no ordinary word. It's a commandment. An imperative. It implies an inviolable role of behavior that has been engraved in granite by the gods for now and all eternity. No excuses accepted. No room for argument. No possibility of defense. And isn't that exactly the behavior of an evil tyrant? ("What! You didn't follow my orders? Silence! I don't want to hear any explanations. It doesn't matter why. To the dungeon with you! Off with your head!")

THE ROLE OF COMMANDMENTS

Perhaps you are saying, "But there have to be *shoulds*. There should be *shoulds*. If there were no rules and laws—no accepted code of conduct—we would have total chaos on Earth. We must cling to some moral, legal, and ethical values or admit that we are no better than wild animals."

That is a reasonable statement. The entire history of the human race proves that we need structure in our lives. But how much structure? What kind of structure? There is a great deal of difference between living in a cottage and living in a cage.

Rules are important, yet sometimes it is necessary to question them. Sometimes circumstances dictate that we revise our code of conduct. Take the Commandment "Thou shalt not kill." Most of us have strong feelings about that one. And yet, don't we modify it under certain conditions? Suppose a maniac were attacking your children—or your neighbor's children—with an ax, and you realized you could stop him by running over him with your car—although it might mean you'd kill him. Wouldn't you step on the gas?

At times we may find that something we consider an absolute must (just another word for *should*) is in conflict with another *should* that we hold just as dear. We may believe that a good citizen should obey the law—and yet find that our community has passed a law we think should not be obeyed. Americans have a long tradition of defying laws they view as unjust. For example, many people were willing to go to jail rather than accept laws allowing racial segregation in this country.

The point is that it is not only possible for us to question and/or modify even the most fervently believed *shoulds* of all time—Commandments that have been handed down to us over thousands of years—it is also possible to question and/or modify other *shoulds* that have been handed down to us by our parents or our community or that we have simply adopted on our own.

THE *SHOULDS* WE CALL OUR OWN

Most of us are not even aware of all the *shoulds* we live by. It's easiest to call to mind the *shoulds* that are imposed by law: You should pay your taxes; you should bring your car to a stop at a red light; you should *not* rob the bank. Yet our personal *shoulds* are equally important to us. Some people feel very strongly that you should make your bed when you get up in the morning, or you must brush your teeth after breakfast and not before. Or the bedroom window must be open at night, even in cold weather. Or children should be seen and not heard. Or an adult child should telephone his or her mother every week without fail. Or a business letter should never have a spelling error in it. Any boy scout can tell you that a scout's list of *shoulds* includes being trustworthy, loyal, helpful, friendly, courteous, kind, obedient, cheerful, thrifty, brave, clean, and reverent.

The *shoulds* we call our own come from a multitude of sources—government, tradition, and religious belief, among others. Sometimes we have no idea where a *should* came from—nor do we stop to consider whether it is still relevant to our lives.

There's an oft-told story about a woman who is showing her daughter how to make a baked ham. "First," she says, "you must cut the last two inches off the ham before putting it in the pan and bake that separately." The daughter asks why. "Because, that's the way it's done," replies the mother impatiently. "That's how my mother taught me, and you know how good Granny's hams taste."

Curious, the daughter goes to Granny and asks her why two inches have to be cut from a ham before it is baked. "I don't know why *you* would do it," the older woman replies. "But the reason *I* did it when your mother was a girl was that I didn't have a pan big enough to hold a large ham."

The *shoulds* you live by every day are important in the area of problem solving because whenever you make plans that will affect your future, you are likely to come up against *shoulds*. You might say, "I want to change my job. I feel I could do much better. But I *should* stay here because the boss has been nice to me."

THE "RIGHT THING"

It's hardly surprising that each of us has firm convictions about what is the "right thing" to do. We start learning *shoulds* very early. When a baby starts to crawl, adults very wisely tell the baby not to touch a light cord, not to climb out of a window. These *shoulds* (or *should nots*) are designed to keep the baby alive and healthy. Thus, we recognize very early that there are good reasons for the existence of rules.

What we may not recognize as easily is that there are often very good reasons why rules should change. It may be dangerous for the baby to touch the light cord, but that doesn't mean a grown man can't touch one without fear that he will pull the lamp off the table and onto his head. But very often we hang on to *shoulds* long past their usefulness. We may continue cutting two inches off the end of the ham even though it makes no sense at all.

THE PATH OF GUILT

Imagine you are riding a horse along a trail that is twenty feet wide. On either side of the path lies trouble—a yawning precipice here, a patch of quicksand there. If your horse steps out of bounds along another stretch of this trail, it will trample on flowers. That's not as bad as tumbling down a cliff or getting sucked into quicksand, yet all the flower lovers will complain about you, and that's not pleasant.

It isn't hard to conclude from this that it makes good sense for you to hold on to your horse's reins and attempt to keep it from straying beyond the borders of the trail. However, since this particular path is twenty feet wide, sticking to the path is not too difficult to manage. You can even relax enough to take in some of the scenery, to sniff the flowers, and to enjoy the pure pleasure of being up there on the horse.

However, let's say the path you are on is only two feet wide. That's a problem because your horse alone is almost two feet wide. In this situation, a great deal of skill and concentration are required to keep horse and rider on the straight and narrow. It's almost inevitable that the horse will put a hoof wrong somewhere. The only question is whether it will be onto flowers or into quicksand. On this kind of trail, a rider can't relax—can't take the time to wave at other riders.

This trail is a metaphor for the rules—legal, moral, and personal—that you agree are important. When you travel on a path twenty feet wide—that is, when you allow yourself some latitude—you can travel through life with comparative ease. But if you insist upon sticking to a path that is only two feet wide, you will either feel anxious—because the horse is getting too close to the edge—or guilty—because it's gone over the boundary again. It's very difficult to enjoy the ride when you go through life in only two modes, anxious and guilty.

You have to ask yourself, "What kind of trail do I want to go down?"

If you insist upon defining every action you take in terms of *shoulds,* you are narrowing the trail and making your trip more difficult. If you look at alternatives in terms of what makes good sense—of what would be better—then you widen the trail and make life easier.

Most people believe a good citizen should pay his/her taxes on time. And that certainly does seem to make good sense, because if you don't pay your taxes on time, the government will impose interest and penalties that increase the size of your tax bill.

However, suppose a man who believes in being a good citizen is short of cash at tax time. He has to decide whether to pay his taxes or resolve another financial crisis facing him. He may well decide to use his available funds to get out of that other nontax bind. He thinks it over and concludes that it would be better in the long run to be late paying his taxes, even though it will cost him extra.

If he paid strict attention to *shoulds,* he would pay his taxes on time even if the other crisis ruined him. Or he would feel so guilty about not paying his taxes on time, he couldn't gain any satisfaction from resolving the other problem. But by considering the choice in terms of what would be better, the taxpayer accepted the consequences of his choice—a higher tax bill—and resolved the immediate crisis without feeling undue anxiety or guilt, a clear case of traveling along a twenty-foot-wide trail.

We are not stuck with the same trail for life. If you have traveled a narrow, anxiety-producing path in the past, you can widen that trail by revising your present attitude toward *shoulds*. Our taxpayer can shed long-held feelings of guilt about not paying those taxes on time merely by reconsidering his action in terms of choosing between *alternative consequences* rather than in terms of failure to do "the one-and-only right thing."

WHEN *SHOULDS* COLLIDE

Many of the hundreds—possibly thousands—of *shoulds* we live by seem rather trivial—certainly in comparison to the Ten Commandments. And yet, as you have probably discovered, even the tiniest of your *shoulds* can set off an explosion when it collides with another *should*.

This can happen when what one person believes is different from what someone else believes. A woman may believe a good husband should tell his wife what is bothering him, while a man may believe a real man keeps his troubles to himself. Or one person will believe that if you aren't going to be on time for a business appointment, you must call and say so, whereas another person believes that a phone call isn't required unless you are going to be *very* late.

You can see the potential for trouble if the woman who believes a husband should reveal all marries the man who believes a man should reveal nothing. Or if the person who believes a phone call is not required is making a sales call on the person who thinks that telephoning when you are going to miss the appointed time should have been the Eleventh Commandment.

You can avoid a great deal of the trouble that *shoulds* bring us simply by being aware of the fact that you have *shoulds* and that others may not share the same list.

You can then:

- Try to learn what *shoulds* the other person holds dear. You may decide it is to your advantage to accommodate him/her. The salesman, for example, may continue to feel that making a phone call when he is only going to be ten minutes late is a waste of time, but decide to waste the time rather than offend his customer.
- Communicate your *shoulds* to those with whom you have a relationship so that you can work out some kind of compromise. It doesn't make sense to pass laws and then keep the laws a secret. It doesn't make sense to expect others to conform to your code of *shoulds* and never let them know what the code contains.

Consider the story of Sarah and Ted, two young people who had become good friends, and who saw in each other the possibility of a permanent relationship. When both made plans to attend the same weekend conference, each saw it as an opportunity to further their romance and achieve a new level of intimacy. Sarah even packed a sexy negligée.

One night, when they came back to Sarah's room after dinner, Sarah said, "I'll just take a quick shower." Five minutes later she emerged wearing the negligée. "I've put out a towel for your shower," she told Ted. "Thanks," replied Ted, looking excitedly at Sarah, "I'll use it in the morning." And with that, Sarah's interest in Ted disappeared. Because, to Sarah, showering before getting into bed was a *should*. She was brought up to believe that one always washed off the grime of the day before touching the sheets. No argument. No exceptions. And so she felt that a man who didn't shower before bed was . . . ecccch . . . dirty. To Sarah, dirty was disgusting. And disgusting is not romantic.

Sarah's *should* wrecked her weekend—and the possibility of a long-term relationship with Ted. The problem was not the *should* itself. There's nothing wrong in believing that you should shower before going to bed. The problem was that Sarah didn't realize how important this particular *should* was to her—and didn't communicate that fact to Ted.

She might have done so in a number of ways. She could have been coy and simply asked him to join her in the shower and scrub her back. She could have been inventive and said that the touch of a guy who has just come from a shower really turns her on. She could have been frank and told Ted she doesn't enjoy going to bed unless both partners have showered.

Instead, she broke up a budding romance with an otherwise appealing young man who never knew what he'd done wrong. She is left with another "might have been if only" Ted had done what he "should"—when she never gave Ted a chance to make a choice.

This happens over and over again. Marriage counselors tell of wives who felt unloved and unappreciated because a husband didn't remember to send a card on their wedding anniversary. Or a husband is upset because his bride didn't send a birthday card to his mother. He thinks this means she doesn't like his mother. Yet in each case, the lack of a card may only mean that someone from a family that believes one *should* send cards to mark occasions and anniversaries has married someone from a family where that particular *should* doesn't exist. If both sides understand how they differ, they are more likely to work out a mutually agreeable policy on card sending. The hurt feelings will evaporate.

This brings us to what we might call the First Law of *Shoulds,* which is: "Just because you believe something is the right thing to do doesn't mean everyone else believes that, too."

And that means you cannot assume that the rule book in your mind exists in everyone else's mind. Try to learn about other people's *shoulds* when you are developing a relationship of any kind with them. And let others know what your *shoulds* are, too.

It must be said that merely knowing each other's *shoulds* doesn't mean all conflict will be instantly resolved. A woman who feels she should work late hours in order to get ahead in her career may find herself in conflict if she is married to a man who feels a woman should put home and husband before career. But learning each other's *shoulds* at least allows each partner to analyze the choices that can be made and to decide which would be better. Accommodation by one side or the other? Ending the marriage? Compromise? When you think in terms of choice, you can think in terms of setting goals and solving problems. When you assume that *your shoulds* are the only ones that exist, you tend not to think at all.

There is also a "Second Law of *Shoulds*." This one says, "Even if you are sure you know the 'right' way to do something, it doesn't mean that is the 'best' thing to do."

After all, as we mentioned before, you may sometimes decide that the "best" thing to do is to respect someone else's *should,* even though you know that the other person is "wrong." As in, "Okay, I'll call, even though I shouldn't have to because I'm only going to be ten minutes late." "Okay, I'll send a card because it's important to him, even though I think it shouldn't be important to him." Or, "Okay, I'll do things the way the boss wants them done, even though I know things shouldn't be done that way."

There may be times when you will ask another to respect *your shoulds,* even though you know that they think *you* are "wrong."

QUESTIONING YOUR *SHOULDS*

Just as you find that it may sometimes be a good idea to recognize that others may have beliefs that are different from yours and to respect those beliefs—even if you think they are wrong—it can also be a good idea to question your *own* internal set of commandments. You may want to consider the possibility of modifying one of your rules, or changing your mind entirely about it.

A woman whose son committed suicide could not forgive herself because she believed she should have been able to prevent it. Her personal book of rules says:

1. A good mother should know what her child is thinking at all times.
2. A good mother should be able to kiss any hurt and make it better.
3. A good mother should not allow any harm to come to her child.

Did she violate those rules? Yes. Guilty. Guilty. Guilty.

But are those rules reasonable? She does not allow herself to ask that question. That's what *shoulds* do to us. They don't allow us to ask questions. They don't allow us to give ourselves a fair trial. They don't allow us to present a defense of any kind, or even to debate the severity of the sentence to be imposed upon us. They don't allow us to analyze, to consider, and to apply common sense. That is why we must eliminate the word *should* on those occasions when we desperately need the aid of our common sense.

How do you do that? Simple. You simply replace the words *I should* with *It would be better if . . .* (Or, *I should have* with *it would have been better if . . .*)

It makes an enormous difference.

See for yourself. Try this: Write a list of *shoulds*. Write down every *must* engraved in your mind that applies to friendship, family, religion, work, sex, sexual roles, business dealings, politics, personal habits, etc. Write down all those things you know you should have done, or should not have done, in the past. What Commandments have you broken? What are you feeling guilty about? You'll probably have writer's cramp before you get to the end of this list.

Now, from that long list, pick those *shoulds* that are most important to you, like this:

—"I *should* call my mother once a week."
—"I *should* have taken that job offer I had last year."
—"I *should* have married Max, who became a millionaire."
—"I *should* have forced my father to take his medicine."
—"I *should* have been a better mother."
—"I *should* have made contacts while I had the opportunity so that I would be in a better position today."
—"I *should* have sold the stock while it was still possible to make a profit."

Now, on another page, take all those things you claim you should do or should have done and insert them at the end of this sentence:

It would have been better (or easier) if I . . . (Or: in the case of a present *should: It would be better if I . . .*)

You will find that just by changing the wording, you open yourself up to the kind of questioning that the word *should* so effectively discourages.

Here's an example:

If you say, "I should call my mother every week," and then don't call her, you'll feel guilty. But feeling guilty may be all you ever do about it.

If you say, "It would be better if I called my mother every week," you can deal with the matter more rationally.

Would it really be better? Why would it be better? "Because my mother would be happier. She'd stop nagging me about not calling her. I'd be reassured that she was healthy."

So why don't you call? Are there reasons for the choice you have made? Are there reasons why not calling seems a better idea than calling? "I don't call because my mother almost invariably launches into criticism of me. We end up fighting and I stay upset for days. Besides, I feel a need for distance, for independence."

Is there some way to work out a compromise so that you call, which you think is a good idea, but she doesn't put you into a terrible funk, which you think is a bad idea? "Maybe I can make a deal with my mother to exchange the promise of regular telephone calls, even if not every week, for the promise of a moratorium on criticism?"

Sounds good. But what if she doesn't agree? "If she doesn't agree, I probably won't call as often as she'd like. But since she could have done something to encourage my calls, I won't feel so guilty about it."

Here's another example:

If you say, "I should have married Chris," but you didn't and Chris is now married to another, you are wasting energy since it is too late. Coulda/woulda/shoulda . . . but didn't.

If you say, "My life would be better if I had married Chris," you open the proposition to analysis. Would it be better? How do you know? You just think so, but you have no proof of what marriage to Chris would have been like. You are free to romanticize your relationship only because you don't know for sure.

Next, even though marrying Chris might have been a better idea at the time you two were going together, is it still the better idea today? Maybe he'll decide that he, too, made a mistake in his choice of mate and he'll divorce her and find you. But, of course, even if that happens, Chris will not be the same man today that he was at nineteen. Today, he is thirty-nine, the father of three. Do you still have the same interests in common?

Whenever you come up against a *should*—either one from the past or one that pops up as you try to come to a decision about what action to take right now—*rephrase it!* Change *should*—the command that has no alternative, to *it would be better*—and then apply your common sense to answering these questions:

• Why would it be better?
• What alternatives exist?
• What are the consequences of choosing an alternative?
• Would one of those alternatives be better?

You can apply this technique to *shoulds* of past, present, and future. You can take any command and turn it into a choice.

CHOICES HAVE CONSEQUENCES

When you invoke a *should,* you are saying that the consequences that will result from breaking it are too terrible to contemplate. When you think in terms of making a choice, you may well decide, after contemplating the consequences, that they are indeed terrible. But you may also decide they are not as terrible as the alternative.

If in the past you made a wrong choice—if you caused pain to others or yourself—you may well decide that some form of repentance and reparation are required. That, too, is a choice of what would be better. If you are going to pay for your mistake, how are you going to pay? Is it better to wallow in endless regret or to take some action to make amends?

Sally came to the Center for Cognitive Therapy overcome with guilt because she had gotten involved in an extramarital affair. "It was a betrayal of my husband," she said. "A betrayal of my religious beliefs." She felt so guilty about violating this important *should* that she couldn't enjoy anything. She could not get her transgression out of her mind. She was sure it meant—indeed, should mean—the end of her marriage, although that wasn't what she wanted.

Sally learned to say, "It would have been better if I had not made the choice to have an affair." She thought about why she had made that choice. Why did it seem the better idea at the time? It turned out that Sally's husband is a good man but emotionally cold and undemonstrative. In the period before Sally met the man with whom she had an affair, her husband was even more withdrawn than usual. Sally was feeling angry and alone. ("He *should* provide the emotional support I need.") Thus, when she met a man who offered her emotional and sexual comfort, she accepted it.

By avoiding all the *shoulds,* Sally is better able to focus on what options she has for the future rather than alternating between anger at what her husband didn't do (and how she paid him back by having an affair) and guilt over having the affair (which could mean the end of the marriage.) She was able to focus instead on the relationship. It would have been better, she concedes, if she hadn't had an affair. It would have been better if she'd been more sympathetic to her husband's problems. It would have been better if he'd been able to give her the emotional support she needed. That kind of thinking leads to a problem-solving question: "Is there something we can do to better meet each other's needs so that we can save our marriage and neither of us will opt for an affair again?"

HEADING DOWN THE TRAIL

As you ride on down the trail of life, you will not be able to avoid conflicts between your *shoulds* and those of others. You will undoubtedly have to face the consequences of the choices you make. But one of the most important choices you will ever make is the width of the trail you travel. Will you encase yourself in so many *shoulds* that you are forever stepping off the path and into anxiety, conflict, and guilt? Or will you broaden your options by conceding that *what is better* may change or be modified once all the facts are in.

Chapter Nine

THE URGE TO GET EVEN

It's bad enough that we have to cope with the results of our own missteps and mistakes in life without having to deal with all the forms of unhappiness that can be brought upon us by the actions—or inaction—of others. But that's the way it is. Some of the problems that face us are somebody else's fault—or at least we think they are.

When you say to yourself, "My life would be better today if So-and-so had done what he or she should have done—and easily could have," you may well find yourself locked into thinking of ways to retaliate, to get revenge, get even, or obtain some measure of "justice."

Just thinking about the grief, or even the mere inconvenience, another person has caused you can get your stomach juices sizzling. Thinking about the problems that could have been avoided if only that other person had even a grain of decency, honesty, intelligence, or sense of fairness is enough to bring those juices to a boil.

The object of your ire could be a total stranger who has carelessly taken up two parking spaces in a crowded lot, or the car-driving turtle who blocks the road just when you are late for a train. It could be the jerk at work who has given the promotion to somebody who doesn't deserve it, or the spouse who is simply being impossible, or the children who are ungrateful, or the parents who never understood anything at all, or the nasty neighbor, or the unctuous official, or any number of others who afflict us.

The gut aches to do more than just "take it lying down." The desire for revenge is a truly universal feeling. We enjoy it vicariously when we take in movies like *Rambo* or *Death Wish,* in which the good guy wipes the bad guys from the face of the earth. Yeah! Don't we wish that we, too, could so effectively exact "an eye for an eye" from everyone who offends us, who betrays us, who causes us pain? We are only asking for simple justice, after all. Is that too much to ask?

Well, in large measure, it depends on just how much trouble you are willing to take to balance accounts. It depends on how much additional pain *you* are willing to suffer in order to make sure the other side suffers, too. And it depends on whether what you are doing *is,* in fact, making the other side suffer—or just causing *yourself* that additional pain.

It is possible to get so tied up in your desire to get back at someone who has wronged you that you are unable to begin a new life for yourself. Admittedly, some people don't care about that. They feel that "seeing justice done" is more important than their own personal happiness or the happiness of their family. Some people think that there is only one question to be asked when someone has harmed you: "What punishment is deserved?"

But for most people there are two questions: "What punishment is deserved?," and "What course of action is best for me to take?"

THE HISTORY OF REVENGE

Human beings have debated both of those questions for centuries. In very ancient times people believed that a victim of violence could never rest unless his or her kin exacted vengeance not only against the person who committed the wrong, but against that person's entire family. But eventually people came to realize this could not go on without endangering all of human existence. They came to realize that personal revenge-taking tended to be an unending process— you hurt me, so I hurt you back, so you attack my family, so I attack your family, and so on.

A search began for ways to limit revenge. The Old Testament admonition about taking "an eye for an eye, a tooth for a tooth" was a major limitation in biblical times, because it meant that if someone put out your eye, you were entitled *only* to put out his eye—not to kill him or his family. In the New Testament, Christ suggests interrupting the cycle of revenge by simply "turning the other cheek." The prophet Muhammad suggested the idea of "blood money"—i.e., financial payment—in lieu of physical retribution.

Slowly, over time, people came to believe that if justice required revenge, the State, rather than any individual, should handle it.

Slowly, over time, people realized that only a movie super-hero can exact violent revenge and not have to worry about suffering more than a heavy sweat in the process. Millions of bullets come Rambo's way, and not one touches him. But we know that's not real. We know that in the real world, anyone who seeks violent revenge risks ending up in jail. We know that, at the very least, exacting violent revenge means trouble.

Many people got an emotional release from the story of Bernhard Goetz, who, having been mugged twice, took out a gun and shot four teenagers he thought were threatening him on the New York subway. But even those who applauded Goetz for "fighting back" and who thought it "served those kids right" wouldn't necessarily have wanted to be in Goetz's shoes afterward. He was arrested. He was sued. He incurred heavy legal bills. He was convicted on a minor criminal charge, even if not a major one, and received a jail sentence and a fine. And, of course, if he'd been less steady in his aim, he might have hit some other, totally innocent fellow passenger on the subway.

WHEN IT HURTS YOU MORE THAN IT HURTS THEM

Of course, most of us who are concerned about getting even for slights, hurts, and unfair treatment are not thinking in terms of taking a gun and shooting somebody. There are many, many forms of revenge. Yet to an astonishing degree we find—just as our ancient ancestors did—that revenge of any kind can end up hurting the revenger much more than it hurts the revenger's targets. Some people harm themselves beyond belief in their desire to "get back at" and "get even."

Hard to believe?

Let's review some of the most common behavior associated with the human need to get even. Let's see if one or two of these sound familiar to you.

The Wishful Dreamer

It is often the case that when we feel wronged, we don't actually *do* anything to cause our enemy harm, but we *think* about doing so. We think about it a great deal. In our fantasies, of course, we are all superheros—zapping opponents at will. How lovely it is to imagine our foe stepping into an open manhole, falling overboard, being struck by lightning. Perhaps you imagine yourself becoming the president of the company and firing that hardhead who has given you a bad time. Or you can picture yourself being asked to deliver a speech at the university that didn't accept you—and loftily turning them down. Or maybe you imagine snubbing some lout—preferably in a public arena. Take that!

This kind of wishful dreaming can be a wonderful release valve—but it can also be a trap. Thoughts of revenge can become a problem if they become a *major preoccupation*—that is, if thinking about "What can I do to hurt X" or "What I'd like to see happen to that no-good lowlife" stops you from thinking about "What's next for me?" A fantasy is fine when it occupies a corner of your mind. But when you begin living in that corner *most of the time,* it's time to get out.

You must ask yourself, "Do my revenge fantasies make me feel better—without incurring the cost of a lawsuit or the risk of going to jail? Or am I spending *so much time* plotting vengeful acts against someone else that I haven't had time to think about making a new and better life for myself?"

The Procrastinator

Putting off until tomorrow (or never) something that we were supposed to do today is something that most of us do occasionally. And there are many reasons why you would procrastinate. But certainly one of the reasons some people procrastinate is revenge.

—A wife who resents her husband's overbearing attitude deliberately puts off doing the laundry until he has run out of shorts.
—A husband who claims his wife is always nagging him always manages to find a reason not to fix the leaky sink he knows is driving her crazy.
—An employee never gets around to producing the report the boss has asked for because he thinks the boss has demeaned him by giving him such a stupid assignment in the first place.

In each case, the "victim" is retaliating—quietly and non-violently—by not doing something the other person wants done. Is this successful revenge? Probably not. You just can't guarantee that your revenge won't be followed by their revenge. What if the husband becomes so angered by the lack of clean shorts that he becomes even more insufferable than ever? What does the wife do next? And what will he do next? In other words, if the object is to convince the husband to modify his behavior, is revenge the best way? Or is it more likely to add to the troubles of the revenger?

Will the husband who refuses to deal with the leaky pipe as revenge for "nagging" end up with a happier marriage or just a leakier pipe and an angrier wife? And isn't it likely that the employee who "fixes" his boss by failing to turn in the report will end up in a worse fix himself?

This sort of revenge is usually a substitute for a more direct means of resolving anger. The wife who puts off washing her husband's shorts might get better results by talking to her husband directly about what he does that bothers her. She might offer to trade prompt laundry service in return for some specific change in his behavior. It is possible that he could say, "Too bad. I don't care whether or not you are annoyed. I don't plan to change anything I do." In that case, she may consider leaving him. She may consider reshaping their relationship in some other way. But merely "getting back" at him by procrastination resolves nothing—except to fill *her* with helpless rage.

The Dog in the Manger

This popular form of revenge basically takes this position: "I'm not happy, so I'll make sure no one else is, either." The dog in the manger will purposely ruin something that might be of great benefit to himself (or herself) . . . just to deny a benefit to another. For example:

—A young man who feels his parents don't care enough about him fails in school in order to hurt them. He knows that they care about academic success, and that his failure will both embarrass and upset them. He doesn't openly confront them. He "teaches them a lesson" by missing just enough classes to get failing grades. But, of course, in the process of upsetting *them,* he denies *himself* the education that might stand him in good stead in the future. Long after his parents are dead, his determination to embarrass them will be affecting him. Who will be more embarrassed then?

—A man, angry at a court order to pay his ex-wife 50 percent of his income, deliberately takes a job with no future for himself in order to make sure *her* share is half of very little instead of half of a lot. Of course, *his* share is now pretty small, too, and is likely to stay that way. Does this make his life better?

The Scene-stealer

Some people are more dramatic than others in their form of revenge, but the form always remains self-destructive.

—A young woman is angry because her parents are pressuring her to marry the boy next door. "They treat me like a child," she says between clenched teeth. "I'll show them. I'll marry Rocky Road, the head of the outlaw motorcycle gang." Or, "My parents broke up my romance with Ann. Well, they'll be sorry. I'm marrying a woman with a serious dope-addiction problem. Let's see how they like *that*!" Let's see how much *he* likes that. Who is really being hurt here? How sweet is this revenge?

The Suicide

People will frequently say, "I don't care what happens to me. I just want to know that he/she/they will suffer. If that means committing suicide, I'm ready to go. They'll be sorry when I'm gone." Many suicides are hostile acts—acts of revenge.

—A woman allowed her boyfriend to involve her in group sexual escapades that left her feeling humiliated. She went along because he threatened to leave her, and somehow that seemed even more terrible. When finally she could not face the abuse anymore, she decided to kill herself in his apartment. Instead of simply saying, "I think you are a scumbag," and leaving, she was determined to make sure he "faced up to what he had done" to her—by assuring that he would discover her dead body in his bed. She didn't want to just leave, she wanted to leave him with guilt—the gift that keeps on giving.

That assumes, of course, that the scumbag who abused her while she was alive will care at all that she is dead. He had no decent feelings before, why would he have any afterward? Most likely, he'd call the police to come take the body away and then go looking for another girlfriend. Is this worth dying for?

—A young man plotting a vengeful suicide was able to picture the emotional carnage he intended to leave behind. "My mother will break down and my father will be a basket case. Good. Then they'll know they should have treated me better."

His revenge, of course, depends entirely on his parents being upset and breaking down on learning of his death. But that may only be wishful thinking on his part. They might be relieved instead. "It's sad," they say, "but he was so un-happy, maybe it's for the best."

RULES FOR SUCCESSFUL REVENGE

The long and uneven history of revenge indicates that there are certain rules to be followed if one is to retaliate with any degree of success.

1. *The enemy must care about the revenge being taken.*
   If your opponent wants nothing more than to become a martyr, you may be doing him a favor by burning him at the stake.

2. *The revenge should not escalate into continuing warfare.*
   This rule, as we noted before, has stumped revengers for millions of years. It's very difficult to get back at someone in a way that guarantees that that person (or the law) will not then turn around and get back at you.

3. *The revenge should hurt the other person more than it hurts you.*
   This is even trickier, as the foregoing discussion indicates.

4. *If you want your revenge to change your opponent's behavior, the opponent must be aware of it.*
   If the wife who puts off doing the laundry never lets her husband know she is annoyed at him, he may never real-ize she is upset but merely conclude that she is incompe-tent at scheduling laundry. Thus, since he doesn't know she is exacting revenge, he will continue the behavior that so annoys her.

No doubt you can think of some exceptions to these rules. Some people, for example, are able to gain great satisfaction from an act of revenge that the "enemy" does not realize has taken place. A waiter, angry at a troublesome restaurant patron, spits in the patron's soup before bringing it from the kitchen. A homeowner, furious about a truck that was blocking his driveway, lets air out of one of the truck's tires. For this kind of revenge to be "successful," however, it's important that the act *remain* secret. If the chef sees the waiter spitting, the waiter is out of a job. And what other restaurant would hire him? Is the satisfaction of getting revenge on someone who doesn't even know it's happening worth unemployment? If the truck driver comes back while the homeowner is letting air out of the tires, he may have some vengeful ideas of his own.

DECIDING IF IT'S WORTH IT

Of course, the fact that something is difficult to do is not, by itself, reason not to do it. It's difficult to quit smoking, but you may decide to try if you are concerned about your health. It is difficult to run a marathon, but you may do it just because you enjoy it.

It can cost you in time, money, and emotional upset to go to court to testify against someone who has committed a crime, and yet you'd do it because you feel a crime-free society is worth fighting for. No doubt there are many things you feel are worth fighting for, even if the fight is difficult. Whistle-blowers who call attention to the waste of public money or a threat to public health may be well aware that doing this can damage their careers, and yet they choose to follow the dictates of conscience.

What it all boils down to is that, in the realm of revenge, as in any other, *you* must make a choice. What price will you pay to make sure "they" pay?

This is surely a decision that requires some serious thinking through. And yet, too often we rush into this kind of decision—never examining what we are thinking about it. We never ask, "Who is being hurt here?" And, "Is the satisfaction worth the price?"

Here's an everyday example. Bob's wife has not only left him, she has left the kids behind, too. He feels she has "no right" to do this, and he resolves to make her suffer for her "irresponsibility." His thinking goes something like this: "I'll keep the kids away from her. I'll fight her on visitation rights. I'll make sure the kids know what kind of person she is . . . even if it makes the kids cry. Even if later they hate me for saying what I've said. They'll probably get into trouble and it will serve her right for leaving. She'll be sorry then."

When Bob's wife retaliates—making accusations against him in court—he feels even more justified in his vengeful behavior. "See?" he says. "That just proves what I've been saying. She's no good and never was. I'm right to keep the children from seeing her."

Revenge begets retaliation, which begets still more revenge, which destroys innocent bystanders to the battle (i.e., the children who become victims of their parents' revenge).

Is it worth it?

An angry daughter is determined to make her parents suffer because they don't care about her. They don't express affection. They don't express approval of anything she does. Indeed, they don't even seem to *notice* anything she does . . . no matter how deliberately provocative . . . no matter how embarrassing to them (and to her). This proves to her that they are indeed unfeeling monsters and fills her with the determination to find a way to punish them until they see the error of their ways. "What do I have to do," she asks, "to get them to see what they did?"

It may very well be that there is nothing she can do to get them to see what they did. They may be too thick or too well defended ever to see how their indifference has hurt her. Or if they finally see, they may not care.

Now what?

How much effort should this daughter spend in trying to inflict suffering on her parents in retaliation for the suffering she has endured? Will doing this make her happy? Or might she not be better off simply saying, "That pair will never ruin another day for me. They are hopeless. And from now on, I'm going to spend my time looking after my own best interests. I'm going to look to the future, not to the past."

Each person's story is different. But the question for each remains the same: "Is it worthwhile to devote my life to trying to remedy a wrong done in the past?"

CHECKING OUT THE TARGET

In all that we have said so far, we have assumed that the target of your dislike is in the wrong, and you are, as you claim, in the right. But there is always the possibility that blame in your situation should be divided. Or that you may be overreacting.

—Yes, the spouse you are divorcing was not a very good mate. But you bear some responsibility for making a poor choice of mate.

—Yes, you didn't get the promotion you deserve. But did you let anyone know you were interested in a higher position?

—Yes, Joe at work isn't friendly, but then he isn't friendly to anybody. Maybe he has a problem. Maybe he is, as the saying goes, more to be pitied than blamed.

Are you jumping to conclusions about who is hurting you and how much harm they are doing?

DOUBLE-CHECKING

When the urge to hit back comes upon you, as it comes upon us all, think before you act. Write down the advantages and disadvantages of your plan for getting even.

"They want me to graduate, so I won't."

What is the advantage of not graduating? *"They won't like it."*

What is the disadvantage? *"I won't have an education. I won't be able to get the job I want."*

Questions to be considered:

—"Are they being deliberately harmful, or are they just ignorant?"

—"Are they even aware of my plot for revenge?"

—"If they are aware, do they care?"

—"Even if they care, who is being hurt more? 'Them' or me?"

—"Is it worth it?"

"I hate my ex-husband for what he did to me. I think about him all the time. I imagine all sorts of horrible punishments for him. I imagine him asking me to come back and me saying no, never. I imagine him finally getting his comeuppance—maybe he'll get sick. Maybe he'll be fired."

What is the advantage of this dream? *"I feel more powerful when I put this guy down, even if its only in my imagination."*

What is the disadvantage? *"It doesn't change my own social life. I find myself talking about my fantasies, and that turns off other men and bores my friends. Even my family is annoyed with me. While I'm fantasizing, he's enjoying himself and I'm not."*

Is it worth it?

CUTTING YOUR LOSSES

Sometimes you have to learn to cut your losses. If you were selling women's blouses and had a dozen left at the end of the summer season, you would have two choices: put them on sale or put them in storage in hopes of getting full price for them next year. There is no doubt that you won't get as much profit as you hope from choice number one. But the risk of choice number two is that the style of blouses will change before next summer arrives and you won't be able to sell them at any price. You can hang on to the blouses hoping that the style will return someday, but there is a cost to that. The money invested in them can't be invested in new stock that has a better chance of selling right away.

What is true in the retail fashion business is true in other realms of life. No one welcomes a loss, but you may well find that your best move is take a loss and move on. Maybe that means "letting them get away with it"—but maybe it also means letting *you* get away *from* it.

LIVING WELL AS THE BEST REVENGE

A seventeenth-century poet-priest named George Herbert wrote that "living well is the best revenge." And sometimes it is. If the other side had hoped to make you miserable, what more perfect justice can there be than *not* to be miserable?

The desire for revenge can be a splendid motivator. Lee Iacocca has said that the reason he worked so hard to turn

Chrysler Corporation around was to spite Henry Ford, who had fired him as president of Ford Motor Company. Success can be perfect revenge even if the person who put you down never knows about it. A writer tells of being so infuriated by an editor who told her that "your kind are a dime a dozen," she was determined to prove him wrong. And she did—although there is no way of knowing whether the editor ever heard about it. But since she's content with her career, she really doesn't care.

Living well can mean merely getting on with your life. You may already have discovered that while you are getting even, others are getting ahead—and that only makes you feel worse. Living well can mean having a life that is not lived in another person's shadow.

The key question to ask in this matter of revenge is, "What's in it for me?" You can weigh the advantages and disadvantages of revenge just as you can weigh the advantages and disadvantages of taking a particular job. What do you get? What do you give up?

If you get sufficient satisfaction out of making your enemy unhappy—if, indeed, you can be sure you *are* making the enemy unhappy—you may not care how much of your own life you sacrifice in the process. If you get a bigger kick out of blaming others than seeing how you can solve your problems on your own, it's your choice. It is for you to decide whether you would prefer to be bitter or whether it would be better to turn your attention to ways and means of improving your own life. It is for you to decide whether the cause is worth it or whether all you are causing is more trouble for yourself.

Chapter Ten:

COMPARING YOURSELF TO OTHERS

One day you are reading the newspaper and come upon a small article about an old schoolmate who has received a promotion or a terrific new assignment. Or maybe this person from your past is being quoted as a respected expert. Or maybe the article describes his or her marriage or travels.

Whatever it is, it's good news about your old schoolmate. And bad news for you. That's how you feel about it anyway. Not because you have anything against the subject of the article. Not that you wish him or her any ill. It's just that seeing that name associated with something big makes you feel very small. Seeing news of that person's success makes you feel like a failure.

It's bad enough this can happen once or twice. But when you are feeling low about some mistake or misstep or missed opportunity of your past, it seems to happen again and again. You begin to feel that you are permanently parked on the highway of life while others are speeding ahead.

The speeders who set off these kinds of feelings in us don't even have to be people we know. You can get a severe case of the left-behind blues from a total stranger. You might be watching the TV evening news and learn that the new undersecretary of state is thirty-nine years old. And you're forty-three. Or you hear that somebody at your office is leaving to take a much grander job. And you find yourself thinking,

"Why is he (or she) there when I'm still here?" Or perhaps you are jolted by someone who seems to have something that you once had, but have lost. A story of a happy marriage, for example, might hurt you by reminding you of your own divorced state.

Compared to that other person, known or unknown, you find yourself wanting. It's a very unpleasant feeling. Stirred by this uncomfortable comparison, all manner of woulda/coulda/shoulda thoughts start racing unbidden through your mind. "I should be doing that, but I wasted my life. . . ." "I'd be doing that if only I'd . . ." You feel hopeless. You feel sick.

No doubt you've noticed that this turmoil is touched off only by news of certain people—and not others. When you hear about some people, you feel only admiration or pleasure—or you really don't care one way or the other. Do you get precisely the same emotional jolt when you read about (a) your old schoolmate, (b) the secretary of State, (c) the superintendent of schools, and (d) Bruce Springsteen? No, you get a negative effect only from good news about someone with whom, rightly or wrongly, you feel you are in competition. Good news about anyone else is immaterial. You can unabashedly admire the good job that others do and the happiness that others have—*when you don't consider yourself in competition with them.* Famed psychologist William James once said that he didn't care if he met someone who could speak Greek better than he, since he didn't seek to excel in Greek, but if he met someone who knew more about psychology than he did, he was mortified!

The late psychologist Carl Rogers called the image each of us has of ourselves our "ego-ideal." It's part reality, part the way we want to be, part the view we intend others to have of us. Anything that rocks our ego-ideal shakes our self-confidence, upsets our equilibrium.

Do you remember the first time you heard your own voice on a tape recorder? Were you dismayed? Unnerved? If so, you are far from alone. Most of us hear our own voices as nicely modulated, located somewhere in the middle-to-lower sound range. Then you hear yourself on a tape sounding more like Daffy Duck. You don't want to believe it. When opera star Luciano Pavarotti saw a documentary made about a tour he'd taken through China, he commented, "I look like that?" And went on a diet to lose eighty pounds.

Comparing yourself to another with whom you identify in some way can provide a similar kind of rude shock to your ego-ideal, that is, to your sense of who you are and how others see you.

MAKING COMPARISONS

In this society, comparing is a cultural trait that is instilled in us from earliest memory. Parents say, "Why can't you be as quiet as your brother?" Or, "Johnny down the street doesn't behave this way." Or, "If your cousin Nancy can do it, you can do it, too."

Teachers divide us into three reading groups: the robins, the bluebirds, and the pigeons. Probably the pigeons are slow learners.

Most business organizations reinforce their hierarchy in very visible ways. The boss has a corner office with two windows. The second-in-command has a corner office with *one* window. The pecking order of the rest of the staff might be established by the height of wall partitions: desk high for secretaries, three quarters of the way up for supervisors, ceiling high for department heads.

And on top of all that, the mighty messages of the advertising world reinforce the notion that some of us are winners (users of the product) while others (who presumably use Brand X) are also-rans.

Most people would ágree that there is a positive purpose to all this ranking and comparing. Psychiatrist Alfred Adler wrote that the quest for "superiority" is a major motivating factor in life. We deliberately imitate traits of someone we consider our superior in order to become more like them. Indeed, the very existence of such a role model—someone who proves that it is possible to succeed—can be a very important source of inspiration. We strive to improve ourselves in order to be compared favorably to others. We strive to do the right thing to avoid being singled out as unworthy. And sometimes, as we said before, the desire to "show them" that we aren't as second rate as "they" say can be a more effective call to battle than winning any other reward.

Quite commonly, reports author Ralph Keyes in his book *Is There Life After High School?*, those who are accomplished as adults point ("and point often") to some adolescent humiliation suffered in their high school years as the spur that goaded them to seek success. Actress Sandy Duncan said she felt crushed when she failed to become a cheerleader—only six were elected and she'd come in seventh—but that experience made her determined to seek acclaim on the stage. Tom Bradley reported that his determination to win election as the mayor of Los Angeles had its roots in an unsuccessful attempt to become president of his high school senior class.

But, of course, we also realize that comparing can be harmful as well as helpful. Not everybody reacts to negative comparisons in the same way. Suppose, for example, that your father had a habit of always comparing you unfavorably to your older brother. You say you won a prize. He says your brother just got a big promotion. Whatever achievement you can claim, he can point to one of your brother's that is even better. This could well motivate you to excel in order to "show him," in order to prove to him (even long after he is dead) that you are your brother's equal—or better. However, it is also possible—and just as normal, it must be said—that you might find his favoritism so discouraging that you simply drop out, saying, "What's the use? Nothing I do is any good." Or you rebel in some parent-shocking way.

If negative comparisons can motivate, they can also reinforce feelings of inferiority. A mother who complains that her "miserable kid" only says bye-bye when other babies are speaking full sentences may unwittingly be crushing her child's sense of self-worth. A teacher who ignores all but the "stars" in the class may inculcate feelings of despair and/or resentment among the nonstars. (And that won't necessarily make them feel very friendly toward the "teacher's pets.")

But no matter which way we take them, there is just no getting away from comparisons in this culture. For better or ill, we are a people who relentlessly sit in judgment on ourselves and others, and relentlessly rank and compare. We know who is the most beautiful, the most popular, the most successful, the richest.

Sometimes the comparing will produce the kind of nasty-nice feelings of satisfaction that come when we meet the ex–prom queen and find she hasn't aged as nicely as we have, or we meet the "most likely to succeed" and find we've done more. ("Were it not for the misfortunes of our friends, life would be unbearable," wrote the cynical seventeenth-century French epigrammist François, duc de la Rochefoucauld.) But other times, comparing produces the painful shock of recognition that occurs when you are faced with a human reminder that others have whatever you once thought you could/would/should have—but do not.

A SUBJECTIVE PROCESS

Comparing sounds like a scientific process. But rarely is it so outside the laboratory. When it comes to human qualities, values, and achievements, we tend to measure very subjectively. For example:

1. *We tend to compare ourselves to those who have more, rather than to those who have less.*

   A man who owns a chain of stores and has a personal fortune of $3 million is unhappy because a friend has a bigger chain of stores and a personal fortune of $40 million. He undoubtedly knows that most people would be ecstatic to have what he has now. He concedes he doesn't know how he would spend the additional money, since he lacks for nothing now. Yet he feels he isn't doing well *in comparison to his friend.* He thinks, "If only I'd made better deals, I'd be where he is today." He imagines that others look at him as a failure because he sees himself that way.

   This man may be unusual in the amount of money he has. But he is not unusual in being much more aware of his deficiencies than his assets and accomplishments. Most of us take what we have for granted. We rarely say, "I'm very grateful for the education I have received, because I know it is not available to everyone." We say, "How come I'm not as smart as he is?" We don't say, "How wonderful it is that I can play baseball when others don't have the opportunity." We say, "Why can't I bat .300?"

   It isn't that we aren't exposed to the idea of being grateful for what we have. "I cried because I had no shoes until I met a man who had no feet" is a much-quoted moral lesson. However, a teenager who does not have the precise brand of sneakers considered trendy at school is more likely to recall it as, "I cried because I didn't have the right shoes even though I know others have none." What is true of the teenager is true of most of us.

2. *We tend to see those with whom we unfavorably compare ourselves as larger than life.*

   It's easy to believe that somebody else "has it all"—particularly when we are feeling deprived. Poet Edwin Arlington Robinson made this point in his poem "Richard Cory." As described by Robinson, Cory was an enormously rich, good-looking, and well-educated young man, who was the envy of all who saw him. Yet the punch line of the poem is that this much-envied young man commits suicide.

   The point Robinson makes is not that all wealthy, good-looking people are unhappy and ready to shoot themselves. Indeed, you will not be surprised to hear that several surveys show that good-looking and wealthy people are much more satisfied with their lives than most. The point is that, in individual cases, appearances can be deceiving.

   The parade of celebrities through the Betty Ford Center for treatment of drug or alcohol addiction would seem to indicate that a great many men and women who—to judge from stories about them in the media—appear to be leading golden lives have found their lives to be tarnished. All the stories about Wall Street's high-flying investors were enormously flattering—until it was revealed that some of them were using illegal means to make their money. The gold of those lives went from shiny to shabby overnight!

3. *When comparing, we tend to compare only gains, omitting the losses or costs. We tend to measure only those portions of the other's life we covet, and ignore everything else.*

   Chronic gamblers have a way of remembering exactly how much they have won, while conveniently forgetting previous losses. And chronic comparers are much the same. While it's true that some people have breaks handed to them, most people have to make choices—giving up one thing to get another. Just because we don't know the price another has paid to attain the success we see doesn't prove there was none. Since it isn't the custom to go around complaining about your problems, we may not know if and when personal problems exist.

Phyllis Rose, a professor at Wesleyan University, told a story in *The New York Times* about being so nervous at the start of each semester she had terrible anxiety dreams in which she saw herself showing up for her first class stark naked. She felt at the time that she didn't dare tell anybody about this—for fear they'd think a female so insecure wasn't worthy of the job. But then, one evening, she found herself at a dinner party seated next to a distinguished and respected Yale professor who had just retired. He told her that there were many things he would miss about teaching—but one thing he would not miss: the nightmares he had at the start of every semester in which he presented himself at the podium and discovered he was naked.

Cosmopolitan magazine editor Helen Gurley Brown wrote a book called *Having It All,* in which she gave some practical career advice to women who aspire to be as successful as she is. And she made it plain that her formula for "having it all" was not necessarily one that would satisfy everybody. Her career keeps her on the East Coast, while her husband's equally high-powered career keeps him on the West Coast, so they meet only on weekends. The Browns have no children. Not every couple would view that arrangement as "having it all." *Chacun à son gout,* as the French say. Each to his own taste.

COMPARING YOURSELF FAIRLY

It is hard to make a fair comparison if you insist on putting your thumb on the other fellow's side of the scale or if you omit information that might lend weight to your side of the balance. Yet when you are in a woulda/coulda/shoulda frame of mind, you tend to do both of these.

1. *You may see the positives in another person's life—but insist upon discounting any positives in your own life.*
   Someone tells you that you are doing a good job and you say, "You're just saying that to make me feel good."

   It's possible that the person *is* only saying that to make you feel good. But it is also possible that the person is saying it because it's true. A pound for your side of the scale.

   It is also possible that someone who judges you harshly may be wrong. This person may be deceived by appearances. Suppose the passenger sitting in the next seat to you on an airplane spills his chocolate pudding in your lap. Are you going to wear a sign as you get off the plane saying IT WASN'T MY FAULT?

   You may simply be assuming that others have a negative opinion of you with no proof at all that this is the case. For example, you may like to go home every night and watch TV, but worry that other people will think you are boring. Do you know whether or not *they* watch TV?

2. *You establish a time line for events.*
   When you compare yourself to others, you probably are not comparing yourself to Grandma Moses, who started a career as an artist when she was past eighty—or to couples who fall in love for the first time in the Old Age Home. No, you are probably comparing yourself to people who are younger than you are or who are accomplishing the goals you seek in a shorter period of time. You have established an arbitrary time line that says, "By this

time I should be married, by this time I should earn so much, by this time I should have achieved such and such." Thus, you compare yourself with the *shoulds* of the time line as much as with live competitors who seem to be following that schedule. And you rule out the possibility of getting satisfaction from any accomplishment that might either take longer or occur when you are older than your "rival." But which is really more important? *When* you get something—or *whether* you get it?

3. *You denigrate your own choices.*
   Suppose, for example, you decided to become a schoolteacher while your best friend opted to become an attorney. Now, your friend is a partner in a major firm and rolling in cash, while you are wondering whether you'll have to go on strike to get a raise. When you see your friend, in his BMW, five-hundred-dollar suit, and Caribbean tan, you feel like a loser. "That's what I should have," you say. "And I could have had all that. If I had gone to law school, I would be rich today.

   Stop. Is everything you say true?

   —Do you want *all* of the life your friend lives today— and has lived since you made your career choices—or just your friend's current income?
   —Do you want the income for the pleasures it provides, or because you feel others look down on you for not being rich? Or to put it another way, Is this what *you* want, or what you think others think you *should* want?
   —Are you allowing your wistful yearnings for more money or status to block out aspects of your life that please you?

If you insist on looking back, are you looking back accurately?

—Is it true that you could have gone to law school?

—If you could have gone, did you want to, then? Or did you choose to become a teacher because that field interested you more than law?

—How do you know you would be rich today if you had gone to law school? Not every lawyer is rich. If you aren't rich, would you rather be a teacher or a lawyer?

—How do you know you would be alive today if you had gone to law school? Remember that if you change one fact of your past life, it's likely other facts of your life would be different today, too—possibly including the length of it.

Dr. Aaron T. Beck, in his book *Love Is Never Enough,* tells the story of a couple whose marriage was in trouble because the wife compared her husband to the high-powered, high-earning husbands of her friends and found him lacking. He was lazy, she thought. He didn't care about anything. He didn't take life seriously enough.

Beck asked the woman to list what she had found appealing about this terrible man when they first met. She said he was easygoing and relaxed. He didn't criticize her as her parents did. He had a wonderful sense of humor. And those traits, she said, were still very important to her. Could it be, Beck asked, that in comparing her husband to others, she was simply interpreting all his positive qualities in a negative way—while interpreting the negative qualities of others in a positive way? In other words, was her husband "easygoing" or "lazy"? Did the fact that he didn't criticize her mean he didn't care? If he were as serious as those others, would he still have that wonderful sense of humor? Was she willing to give up the qualities that had attracted her in return for a more serious, hard-driving, critical man with a higher income? She decided she loved her husband just as he was.

RECHECKING THE COMPARISON

The first step in dealing with comparisons that leave you feeling rejected and dejected is to simply recheck the comparison, keeping the typical errors of comparison in mind:

—Are you giving too much credit to your competitor and too little to yourself?
—What do you know about the other person? How accurate is your information? How complete?
—Is there any other way to interpret what you know? Is it possible that what seems wonderful is not so good? Is it possible that what seems terrible is not so bad?

RECHECKING THE CONCLUSION

Let us assume that, having checked, you discover that you were right the first time. You really have missed out. Others have passed you by. You did indeed make the wrong choice or had rotten luck or were badly treated by another. Your competitor's life is indeed wrought out of gold, yours is lead. Your ego-ideal is not just teetering, it's down.

Now what?

Do you endlessly ruminate about what led you to come up short in your comparison? Do you simply review the steps you took versus the steps you might have taken? You already know that won't make you feel any better.

Do you escape into fantasy like the fictional Walter Mitty, who, upon seeing someone he admired, lost himself in a dream of becoming that person? Do you simply imagine yourself as an undersecretary or a famous actress or half of a loving relationship or whatever? You already know that won't be satisfying for long.

Or, do you do something—take an action—that will add some weight to your side of the scale?

"I'd like to do that," most people say, "but . . ."

Usually, the "but" is that there is nothing that can be done now to overcome the distance between where you are now and where you would have been, could have been, or should be. . . .

And that may be true.

You may be right that you are never going to be as successful as your "competitor" is now—given your late start. *But you can be more successful than you are now.*

ALL-OR-NOTHING REASONING

It generally happens when our ego-ideal is feeling bruised and battered that our brain shifts into an all-or-nothing mode. We seem to feel we have to have everything that those others we envy have—and nothing less will do.

It isn't enough to shift out of "park" and get back on the highway, we have to know that we will catch up with those who have gone ahead. And if that doesn't seem possible, we refuse to move at all.

A million excuses come to mind. "I don't want to take orders from somebody younger than I am." "I don't want to be an understudy—I want to be a star." "It would be humiliating to me to go back to school at my age." In other words, you feel you have to start off where the other person is now, no matter what.

That's all or nothing reasoning.

—"If I can't have what he or she has now, I'll settle for nothing."

—"If I can't have it right away, without struggle and effort and cost, I'll settle for nothing."

—"If I can't be *guaranteed* that after I struggle, make an effort, and pay the cost, I'll have everything I want and more, I'll settle for nothing."

—"If I can't be sure that the person I envy now will end up envying me and that I'll be able to stick my tongue out and say, 'So there,' I'll settle for nothing."

With this mind-set, what generally happens is, of course, nothing.

ESCAPING THE COMPARISON TRAP

The key to getting out of the comparison trap is to simply change the comparison. If you insist on comparing what you have now with what the competition has now, you may well lose—and stay miserable.

But if you decide you will compare what you have now with the life you may be able to have in the future, given some effort, then you may be able to make a difference.

Yes, you may have to make compromises. If you desire to acquire status symbols like a Rolex watch when you earn a Timex salary, you may have to decide what you will sacrifice to get it. Yes, you may have to make do with even less—if you switch jobs, if you go to school, if you leave home, whatever—in order to reach your goal. The comparison to keep in mind is whether your life is—or will be—improved over what it was like before. The grass may always be greener in the other fellow's yard, but that doesn't mean you have to sit out your life on a rocky patch with no grass at all.

Chapter Eleven

LOST LOVES AND WRONG LOVERS

In the pantheon of past mistakes and missed opportunities, surely a special niche is reserved for the anguish of thwarted love. The poets who call love both "the sweetest joy and wildest woe," who question whether it causes "more of pain or pleasure" recognize the unique hold love has on our lives.

When we seek love, we are more vulnerable—having shed the armor we wear for ordinary encounters. We are more pressured—living in a society that holds to the same standard as Noah's Ark: Please proceed in pairs. How many songs have we heard that send out this same message: "You're nobody till somebody loves you"?

The hurt we feel seems doubled . . . tripled . . . when an intimate relationship—or the hope of one—dissolves. It is no wonder, then, that love gone wrong is so hard to forget. The temptation to woulda/coulda/shoulda thinking can be overwhelming.

When all you can think about is what might have been done differently to win someone's heart, to prevent a breakup, to avoid the terrible pain of rejection, it is all too easy to fall into a pattern of behavior that, in effect, places your heart behind an impenetrable barrier.

For example: You may decide that you are "not worthy" to be significant to another. You may say to yourself, "I'm just inadequate, I'm not cut out for love. I should have known better than to even try."

Or you might speculate endlessly about what it was the other wanted that you did not supply. "If only I'd been smarter." "If only I'd shown more interest in baseball." "He probably thought I was neurotic."

Or you might draw protective cover over your heart. "No one will ever hurt me like *that* again."

Or you might lose yourself in your anger and your desire to get back at someone who hurt you. "I can't rest until I feel he (or she) is suffering as he (or she) has made me suffer." You might decide to devote your energies to winning your ex-lover back merely for the satisfaction of saying, "Good-bye. Now I don't want you."

Or you might romanticize the love you lost to such an extent that no one you meet now—or will meet in the future—lives up to your expectations. "I would like to meet someone, but there is nobody out there. Oh, if only John were still here."

There are satisfactions to be gained from these reactions. You may feel your dignity is salved. You can protect yourself from the possibility of enduring a similar hurt in the future. You can enjoy the modest satisfactions that fantasy provides. But what you must ask yourself is, "Is this enough? Is this what I really want?"

BARRIERS TO LOVE

You may not have asked yourself those questions because, as is often the case, you may not *realize* you have erected barriers to love. The walls have gone up around you, but you may not be aware that they are there. We humans seem to have developed an infinite variety of ways to allow past heartbreak to govern our present and future.

Consider just this small sampling:

The Married Man

When twenty-eight-year-old Katherine was nineteen, her fi-
ancé, Tim, broke off their engagement just before the
wedding. Since then, the only long-term relationship she has
allowed herself is with Norm, a married man. She admits
that Norm may never leave his wife and that she is unhappy
with a relationship that exists solely at his convenience—
never hers. But she says, "At least I have some love in my
life."

She would much rather have the kind of love she is sure
she would have had with Tim, if he hadn't had "crazy" second thoughts, but . . . deep down, she is afraid that if she
seeks that kind of love again, she might be rejected again.
She realizes that Norm may not marry her, either, but she
finds his "rejection" easier to bear because she can tell herself
(lie to herself?) that he is remaining with his wife only "for
the sake of the children."

In return for this ego-protection, Katherine has cut herself
off from the possibility of finding the total two-way relationship she really desires, and sentenced herself to a lifetime
of wondering what would have been if Tim had married her,
or if Norm were not married.

The Polished Image

Peggy is thirty-nine and single. At twenty-five, she fell in
love with Eric, who seemed right for her in many ways—
except that he was of a different religion. This didn't bother
Peggy very much, but it bothered her parents a great deal.
"Please don't do this to us," they said. And the romance
foundered.

Peggy has since thought she should have run away with
Eric. She is sure now that they would have worked out their

differences. But it's too late now. He has married someone else. She has dated others, but no one has measured up to the love that was "denied" her. The life she and Eric would have had together held a promise no one else can fill.

Peggy has saved Eric's picture and the crush-dried souvenir of a flower he gave her. She doesn't know what Eric is like today, yet she remains convinced that she would be happy—and the mother of teenagers—if she hadn't listened to her parents . . . if she had been braver. The men she meets now are too boring, too bald, and with each passing year more unlike the Eric she remembers. She lives in yesterday and is lonely today.

The Substitute

When Charles fell in love with Stephanie, he really fell hard. When she told him that she cared for him—but "only as a friend"—he understood what is meant by "stabbed in the heart."

Charles finally yielded to the pleas of friends to date other women, but because he is sure he can never fall in love again, he approaches women only for pragmatic reasons. He goes out with one woman who might help in his career, another who would probably "be a good mother" to his children, and a third who is "good in bed."

"I could have made Stephanie happy," he says. "It would have been wonderful. But now all I can do is settle for some-one who is acceptable in one way or the other. Charles's de-termination to "settle for less" proclaims his intention of forever focusing on the life that might have been with Steph-anie.

The Last Chance

Myra is still single at forty-eight. And bitter about it. When she was young, she was besieged by suitors—so many, she couldn't decide among them. In fact, she enjoyed the attentions lavished on her and was content to postpone "getting serious" to another day, another year.

But when Myra finally decided she was ready to "settle down," the suitors seemed to have slipped away. "I should have realized I was letting my chances go by," she says. She is determined not to do that again.

Myra is still an attractive woman, but now her desperation to get married intimidates the men she meets. Many women complain that men move too quickly—that they are only interested in sex and are unwilling to take the time that romance requires. But many men get just as nervous when they feel a woman is proceeding too quickly—toward permanence. Myra's belief that her next chance may be her last chance chases every chance away.

The Walking Wounded

Annette feels the twelve years she was married to Jack were wasted. At thirty-seven, she proclaims, "I gave him the best years of my life—the years when I was young enough to meet others, or to make a career for myself. He took them—and walked out. I could have left him, but I didn't."

Annette can't stop telling people how ill-used she was—detailing at length what Jack should have done—even though others find it boring. Alas, no one loves a whiner even when the whiner is perfectly justified in his or her complaint. When men hear Annette's complaint, some feel a need to defend Jack as a fellow male—even though they don't know him. They listen to Annette's gripes and think, "He was probably right about her. She probably complained all the time. I'd better not risk getting to know her better." Others feel there are more interesting women around than angry, unhappy Annette.

Annette would like to hurt Jack—by "letting the world know" about him—but she hurts herself far more.

The Revenge Marriage

"I'll show her," said Mel. "I'm only fifty—I have position, I have money. I'll find somebody else. Somebody better-looking, too. Ha-ha." And he does. He quickly marries a woman who is slimmer than his former wife, and half her age, too. But the last laugh is on him, because "showing somebody" who you feel woulda/coulda/shoulda treated you better, is not a sufficient basis for marriage. Mel was so focused on the effect his glamorous new bride would have on his former wife, he didn't discover until it was too late that he and the young woman he charmed into marrying him had very little in common.

The Destructive Duo

Sometimes Francine can still see in Elliot the charm that first attracted her to him, but more often he shows her his cruel and callous nature. Francine thinks of a line from a song: "He beats me, too, What can I do?" He's her man, but not the man she thought he would be when she invited him to move in with her.

Francine is sure that if only she had been more understanding of Elliot, more giving, maybe less talkative, their relationship might be closer. She isn't really sure what went wrong . . . she is sure only that she could have satisfied Elliot if she were "more of a woman."

When she thinks of asking him to leave, she thinks about his good points (few though they seem to be) more than his bad ones. She tells herself that something is better than nothing. It's too late to do anything now, she thinks. "If I leave, I'll be lonely." So she stays and is unhappy and abused.

The Self-Reject

Lindsay is always on her guard when meeting people. Her parents complain all the time about how fat she is. "If you had stayed slim—and you could have," they say, "you would be married now, because you have such a pretty face."

The result of this "helpful criticism" is that Lindsay's assessment of her own worth is a great big zero. She feels her days of being attractive are behind her now, and no one could possibly love her. If someone says, "You look nice," she thinks, "He doesn't mean it. He's just being polite. If someone says, "I like you," she wonders what is *really* on his mind. Lindsay never gives anyone a chance—and therefore never gives herself a chance.

All of these scenarios—and this is far from an inclusive list—involve people who are not content. They involve people who are allowing the past to determine their present and block their future.

MAKING LOVE HAPPEN

"Some enchanted evening," says the song of that name, "you will see a stranger across a crowded room." That stranger, presumably, will be the love of your life.

It's possible, of course—but only if you are in the crowded room in the first place—not alone somewhere thinking about what woulda/coulda/shoulda been your life today if only . . .

Love, like any enterprise, has to be helped along. It rarely just happens. It rarely comes to people who are sitting all

alone thinking about love lost and chances missed. It comes
to those who are willing to say, "I'd like to find someone
with whom I could be happy—and I'm willing to give that
someone I could love a fair chance to be found."

That means thinking clearly about love as a project. When
you are upset about love gone wrong or a wrong lover, you are
very likely to fall into the habit of thinking negatively about
your possibilities. You are likely to commit one or more of
those all too common, all too human errors of thinking.

HOW THE ERRORS OF THINKING APPLY TO LOVE

Let's run through the many ways that a broken heart causes
our thinking process to go astray:

1. All-or-Nothing Thinking

All-or-nothing thinking says that I must meet the right person right away. If the person I meet is not perfect in every
way, there is no point in pursuing a relationship.

All-or-nothing thinkers will walk into a party and say,
"There's no one here I'm interested in meeting." Then they
leave. If it isn't the party that brings them perfect love, then
it is nothing.

They do not consider that there might be someone there
who knows someone they'd be interested in meeting. They
don't consider the fact that a party may just be fun for its
own sake.

All-or-nothing thinkers reject anyone who has a known
flaw—he's bald . . . he doesn't have great clothes . . . his
occupation is boring. And they therefore never find out
whether that flawed person has dozens of attributes that will
make that flaw pale into insignificance.

All-or-nothing thinkers are not realistic. If you are an average person who will be content only if you marry a superstar, you will probably be disappointed.

2. Perfectionism

The perfectionist, first cousin to the all-or-nothing thinker, assumes that to be loved, he or she must not be flawed.

—"I'm going to go to parties after I lose twenty pounds."
—"I'll be happy to meet people after I get a new wardrobe."
—"I plan to start dating after I get a better job."
—"I'll wait until I feel less vulnerable, until I feel better about myself."
—"I don't think I'm ready yet—I don't have a great line of patter. I'll wait until I'm perfect."

But no one is ever perfect. And to wait for perfection is to wait a long time. While you wait, millions of nonperfect people are finding each other.

3. Overgeneralization

The overgeneralizer takes a few negative experiences and says they indicate how things will always be. "It never works out for me," he (or she) says.

Overgeneralizers give up too soon. They will stop looking (although even if you have to meet one hundred people to find one to love, one is all you need). Or they will settle for someone they don't love. ("I'd better marry Hank, because no one else will ever ask me.") The overgeneralizer is the one who says, "All the men I meet are either married, gay, or crazy." If you ask overgeneralizers to write down the names of all the men they have met in the past year, the men are rarely all married, gay, or crazy. They simply didn't appeal for one reason or another—or the overgeneralizer didn't give them half a chance to appeal.

Overgeneralizers also attribute the opinions of one man to all men. If they believe (rightly or wrongly) that a relationship did not work out because a specific man thought they were "too smart" or "too complicated" or "too interested in work" or "didn't have a good enough figure" or any other reason, they will assume that this is the view of all men, and therefore there is no point in trying to meet someone new. They do not credit men with being as infinitely varied as all humans are.

4. Global Labeling

The global labeler is the person who gives up on finding love because other things in his or her life have not worked out. "I never got anywhere in my career," global labelers will say, "so no one could love me." Not everyone who knows how to love cares about careers.

5. Catastrophizing

The catastrophizer always assumes the worst. "He said he can't come to my party. That means he doesn't like me." It could mean he simply can't make it to the party.

A typical catastrophizer is the woman who was so angry when a man who had promised to call her at 10:00 P.M. had not called by midnight, she picked up the phone to call him and tell him that he needn't call her ever again. And she discovered that the line was dead. She had left an extension off the hook. When she finally reached him, she learned he had been calling and getting busy signals for two hours.

A catastrophizer assumes that no matter how bad the present situation is, anything that follows must be worse. Thus, a woman who is going with a man who treats her shabbily hangs on rather than say, "Good-bye, I'm going looking for Mr. Right," because she has convinced herself that she will find only loneliness.

6. Minimizing

The minimizer is most likely to find himself or herself in a compromised situation. The minimizer makes too little of his or her own value ("I may as well settle for this, because who else would want me?"). The minimizer also makes too little of another's flaws. ("I've heard that he is a notorious womanizer, but I know he'll be faithful to me.")

7. Comparative Thinking

Comparative thinkers constantly evaluate themselves and find themselves lacking. Compared to others, they are too short or too tall or too something else. Others have whatever it takes to be happy.

If they are alone, comparative thinkers suffer pangs of loneliness when they see a couple, even though the individual members of that pair might actually prefer to be single again.

8. Uncritical Acceptance of Critics

The person who too easily accepts the put-downs of others is afraid to trust his or her own judgment. A woman like this may feel totally justified in rejecting the sexual overtures of a man she has just met. He correctly points out that she is not a virgin. He says she is cold; he says she is a tease. He accuses her of leading him on. He says the least she could do is invite him in "for a cup of coffee." He is insulting her, and yet she feels guilty. She feels insecure, unsure of herself. He makes his point so aggressively, she assumes he "must be right." She feels a need to placate his demands even when they go against her own wishes. She is not being fair to herself. She must ask herself, "How much do I care what he thinks? What do *I* think is right?"

If several people repeat the *same* criticism, you may want to examine that. If several people say, "You give the impression that you are unfriendly," you may ask, "What is it I do or say that gives that impression?" If several people say, "You are too friendly. You flirt with others so frequently that it is hard to believe you want a serious relationship," you may want to examine that. And you may decide to change your behavior in some way. But that is not the same thing as assuming that every critic is correct. You have the right to do what seems best for you.

9. Selective Editing

The person who selectively edits sees only part of another's personality and behavior. This can mean that you are so focused on one positive quality that person offers—such as wealth or sexual attraction—that you ignore everything else: a legal spouse, a harsh manner, a lack of mutual interests. This can also mean that you are so focused on a single negative quality that you overlook all the positives. You may say, "Marshall usually seems generous, warm, and sweet, but *yesterday* he seemed rather distant. I can't cope with that." When looking for love, it is necessary to look at the whole picture.

Selective editing often enters the picture when, six weeks after breaking up with someone, you haven't met anyone else. Suddenly, you begin remembering that someone's virtues, while forgetting the flaws that made breaking up such a good idea. You then feel you've lost someone whom, if you considered the whole picture, you would really prefer not to find.

10. Disqualifying the Positive

Disqualifying the positive is a variation on selective editing. It means always finding a flaw somewhere. It's saying, "Yes, but . . ." "Yes, that was wonderful, but . . ."

11. Mind Reading

A mind reader says, "I know what he's thinking, there's no point in asking." A mind reader will say, "There is no point in inviting him to my party, he won't come."

The mind reader draws conclusions about the views of others without bothering to check. Thus, a person who over-generalizes by assuming that "men don't like smart women" or "men don't like women with fat legs" is usually also guilty of mind reading. Mind readers will assume that is what any man they meet is thinking—and never bother to check.

Mind readers also believe that others should know what they are thinking without the necessity of telling them. Thus, a mind reader will think, "He should know I'd like flowers—I shouldn't have to tell him. If he really cared, he'd know." The mind reader refuses to say, "I like it when you do such-and-such in bed" (even if that might spur the desired action).

The only way to know whether you have read a mind correctly is to check it out. The only way to be sure someone is reading your mind correctly is to let him or her know what you are thinking.

LOST LOVES AND WRONG LOVERS

12. Personalization

The personalizer "takes everything personally." Every criticism is taken as rejection. If he doesn't like the picnic supper she prepared, it means he doesn't like her. In fact, it could be only that he doesn't like picnics, or ham sandwiches.

13. Fortune-Telling

The fortune-teller carries an internal crystal ball that is always tuned to disaster. The fortune-teller knows, without ever checking anything out, that it won't work, it's too late, there is no point in trying. The fortune-teller knows that there is no point in going to the party because "no one will be there." Yet no one knows the future. No one knows how another person will react until you give that person a chance to react. No one knows what will happen—until it happens.

14. The Should Syndrome

Sufferers of this syndrome are those who claim there is "only one right way" to do anything. Typical is the person who says, "If you want to go out on a date on Saturday night, you must call by Wednesday. If you call me at 'the last minute,' I shall be indignant. That would mean you assume I will be alone. How dare you assume that?"

The end result is that two people who might enjoy each other's company end up alone. Or maybe only one person ends up alone. The caller may call someone else who does not take this *should* so seriously. That person may think, "I would have liked it better if he had called earlier, but since we're both free, why not get together and have a good time?" More flexibility leads to more possibilities.

15. Emotional Reasoning

The victim of emotional reasoning says, "I feel inadequate, therefore I must be inadequate. I feel my situation is hopeless, therefore it must be hopeless. No, I don't intend to do anything that would prove me wrong." Single people sometimes allow themselves to feel inadequate simply by virtue of being single. They believe that "you are nobody until somebody loves you," even though all you need do is look around to spot independent, productive, and contented single people. They might welcome the "addition" of love, but they do not count themselves as losers because they don't have it. And they do not assume that not having love now means that love is never possible.

A ROMANTIC ACTION PLAN

We already know that solving any problem means coming up with an action plan that, even if it will not bring immediate results, will increase the probability of results.

In the case of romance, this means broadening social activities, increasing your circle of friends and acquaintances.

Brainstorm ways of doing that. People will often say, "But I don't like singles bars." Fine. Don't go to a singles bar. Think of a dozen other places, other ways, other possibilities, for meeting people. Ask yourself what is preventing you from getting to those places, finding those other ways—and try to think of ways to get around those obstacles.

Joanna felt that the most comfortable place to meet people would be at a private party where the host or hostess knows everybody. The problem was that no host or hostess had invited her lately.

Joanna decided to have a party herself. That would mean

she wouldn't meet many new people, of course, although she could ask a few friends to invite some of their friends whom she didn't know.

Because she didn't have much money, Joanna decided to have brunch instead of a cocktail party. Liquor is an expensive item. All that is required for brunch is pancakes and coffee. Besides, people don't go to brunches to check out the food—but to check out the people.

The party was great fun even if Joanna did not meet the love of her life there, and she decided to have another. And another. And after the third, one of her friends said, "Next Sunday, come to my house. I'll have brunch." And he did and she met his friends. And then their friends.

Joanna is simply increasing the probability of meeting a special someone by increasing the number of people she meets. And it is important to point out that while she is doing this, she is enjoying herself. Sunday brunches are much more fun than what she used to do—which was sit around thinking about whom she might have married if only . . .

A romantic action plan can involve asking your friends to introduce you to someone. You can't just assume they will think of doing so if you don't say you are interested. A romantic action plan means assuming nothing until you have checked it out.

CHECKING YOUR CRITERIA

It is important to check the criteria you consider important for that special someone in your life.

Make a list of those criteria: age range, income, height, religion, stimulating conversationalist, interest in skiing, etc. Make it as long as you can.

Then pick those criteria most important to you . . . and

think about them again. A list can be very revealing. It can tell whether you are being unrealistic. For example, a woman who says she wants a man who is aggressive in business who will also put *her* needs first is seeking an all-but-impossible combination. Which is more important?

A list may show that although you claim to want a particular quality, you actually are attracted to people who are nothing like that. If you say you want someone kind and gentle, and realize that you seem to be dating people who are cold and aloof (possibly because they are good-looking or have money), you may be setting yourself up for disappointment.

DO ONLY FOOLS FALL IN LOVE?

You know what kind of person you are seeking, and lo, there is someone who, on first impression, seems to be the right one. How willing are you to approach that person?

It is said that only fools fall in love, because love means taking a risk—indeed, it may mean a series of risks. A romantic action plan may require the same attitude that works for an insurance salesman—twenty leads may result in only one sale. You can't take every rejection personally. You may have to be alone before you can find the right person to keep you company.

No doubt about it, love is the biggest risk we take in life. Love does not pop out of a TV set. To find it, we have to be a little foolish, a little exposed. We have to be open to love—and being open means being vulnerable. But if love is what you want, then that is the choice you make.

Chapter Twelve

WOULDA/COULDA/SHOULDA IN EVERYDAY LIFE

Bad habits, as we all know, come in varying sizes and degrees of importance. Smoking is a dangerous habit that can shorten your life, whereas biting your nails is merely an annoying habit that makes your fingers look shorter. No doubt nail biters who smoke know which habit is more important to break—but that doesn't mean they would not feel better about themselves if they could break both.

Woulda/coulda/shoulda thinkers are in the same position. Although this book concentrates on the *major* horrors of hindsight—that is, on woulda/coulda/shoulda thinking that has life-affecting results—it would be hard to ignore the fact that life is easier and much more enjoyable if you can rid yourself of minor "everyday" woulda/coulda/shoulda thinking, too.

PANIC TIME

Everyday woulda/coulda/shoulda thinking may not block your future, but it can definitely get in your way. Here's an example:

You get in your car in the morning, already annoyed at yourself because you dawdled over coffee and got a late start. Now, you run into a detour caused by reconstruction of a bridge. Too late, you remember that you heard on the late TV news just two nights ago about that bridge being closed. AAAAAARRRRGH!

Now, you are really furious. "I should have remembered. Stupid, stupid, stupid! They should do this work at night anyway. Now I'm going to be late, and that will mean (pick one) the boss will be angry/ I'll miss the appointment/the event I want to see will be half over when I get there/the people I'm meeting will assume I'm not coming and leave."

None of these results would be so traumatic that they would continue to gnaw away at you two decades, two years, or even two months in the future. Yet it is entirely possible, in this situation, for woulda/coulda/shoulda thinking to ruin your day.

One way that might happen is if you are so busy being angry at yourself for getting into this situation that you prevent yourself from seeing an "obvious" way out of it. Remember the story in Chapter Two about the bad guys who were stopped by a tollbooth set up in the middle of the desert? By focusing only on the fact of the barrier in front of them, they made themselves unable to see how easy it would be to go around it.

In the same way, you won't calmly and rationally think about the best alternative route to your destination—or the location of a telephone so that you can call ahead and say you'll be late—as long as your brain is locked into automatic woulda/coulda/shoulda thoughts. "I should have left the house ten minutes earlier. . . . I should have remembered this detour. . . . Couldn't they do this work at night? . . . I'll never make it now. I'm going to be late. This is a disaster. I can't believe I did this. What am I going to say? What am I going to do? I just can't believe I'm in this mess." Somewhere around "This is a disaster," you probably drove past a crucial intersection that might have gotten you where you were going.

What if there is no alternative route or telephone to be found—and you do, in fact, have to face the consequences of being late? In this instance, all that your woulda/coulda/shoulda thinking will accomplish is to upset your stomach, ruin your disposition, and put you in a foul frame of mind that is guaranteed to increase your output of stomach acid, put a damper on whatever you manage to do that day, and keep you from restful sleep that night.

You know this is so. But what to do about it?

CONFRONTING YOUR THOUGHTS

You do just what you do with any woulda/coulda/shoulda rumination. That is, you make yourself aware of the thoughts that are running subliminally through your mind and you challenge them.

Are these thoughts accurate?

Are these thoughts reasonable?

Are these thoughts accomplishing anything at all?

Maybe you need to "decatastrophize." If you hear yourself saying that being late will be a disaster, question that. What kind of disaster? How big a disaster? What—honestly, now—is the worst that can happen?

Amy was a cub reporter who had been sent out to cover a fire and got stuck in traffic. She felt panic rising inside her. Tears came to her eyes. "Nobody will ever trust me to get a story again," she thought. "My career is ended even before it's begun." Amy fought to calm herself. She focused her mind on determining exactly how bad her situation was— and realized it might not be as bad as she feared. Why not? Because if this fire were over before she arrived, that would, more likely than not, mean it was a small fire—one that causes relatively little damage. And in that case, the newspaper would not be interested in a story about it anyway. If it were a major, newsworthy fire, it would most likely still be burning when she got there. The firefighters who would have the information she would need about the fire would still be at the scene.

Maybe you need to consider the usefulness of your thoughts. If, indeed, you are stuck in traffic, does it make more sense to spend twenty minutes berating yourself for being stupid, or twenty minutes thinking of ways to solve a problem at work, or twenty minutes observing the interesting humans stuck in the jam with you, or twenty minutes doing deep breathing exercises designed to induce you to relax?

As long as you are going to be late, wouldn't it be better to be still in control of your emotions, rather than arriving so angry you can't remember what you had planned to do in the first place?

The task of becoming aware of your thoughts, analyzing them for errors of thinking, and questioning your conclusions is calming in itself—simply because it interrupts the woulda/coulda/shoulda pattern that leads only to increased anger, anxiety, and angst.

You are not wrong to be annoyed or upset at a frustrating or upsetting experience; it's reasonable to behave like a human being rather than a robot. But it is possible to make a bad situation *worse* by surrendering to woulda/coulda/shoulda thinking rather than trying to calm down and deal with the problem. You will suffer longer than you need to if you allow your thoughts to *increase* your anger rather than coming to terms with it.

PUTTING OFF TILL TOMORROW

Another way we set ourselves up for a woulda/coulda/shoulda dilemma is procrastination—from the Latin *pro* meaning "toward" and *crastinus* meaning "tomorrow." When you panic, you do nothing to resolve the problem facing you because you conclude it's "too late." When you procrastinate, you do nothing to resolve the problem facing you because you tell yourself you will do it "later."

Here is an example of that pattern, which will be familiar to anyone now in school or who has ever gone to school.

On Friday, Cindy's professor announced that an important exam would be held on the following Friday. "No sweat," said Cindy. "That gives me seven nights to study seven chapters. I'll study one a night and make reminder notes that I can review on the morning of the test."

But no sooner had Cindy set up this sensible schedule than she abandoned it. Friends invited her to a party Friday night. "Sounds like fun, and after all," she told herself, "I still have six nights left."

The party was so much fun that Cindy did not get home until 4:00 A.M. The next day she was so tired that she barely got through the shopping, laundry, and other unavoidable chores. She knew she'd never stay awake to study.

"But what the heck," she thought, "I still have five nights left. And besides, tomorrow is Sunday and I can study all day."

On Sunday, Cindy was invited to an afternoon football game. "It ends early," Cindy excused herself, "and I can be studying by six or seven at the latest." At seven, surprise!, friends from out of town dropped by unexpectedly. What could Cindy do? She couldn't just turn them away. And besides (she said to herself), there were still four nights left.

On Monday, the professor unexpectedly assigned a paper that, he said, was to count for half the final grade. Oh, woe! Cindy scrambled to get that done—which took care of all her free time on Monday and Tuesday. On Wednesday, a guy she'd hoped to hear from for months called and asked to see her that night. . . . What could she do?

"I'll stay up all night Thursday and cram," Cindy promised herself. "I'll take a nap after my last class, set the alarm clock for midnight, then get up and study right up until I have to take the test." At midnight, sleepy Cindy reached out, turned off the alarm, and promptly fell back asleep again. Next thing she knew it was 6:30 A.M., and she began wondering whether she might claim to be going to her grandfather's funeral for the third time.

Cindy had set herself up for a stiff round of woulda/coulda/shoulda—"I could have studied, I should have studied, I would have studied if I hadn't had such wonderful excuses for avoiding it."

Everybody procrastinates now and again, and, admittedly, it is not always a problem. Some students routinely put off studying until the last minute, cram all night, pass the test, and do the same the next time. Since that system works for them, they have no need to change it. But some people—like Cindy—not only wait until the last minute, they let the last minute pass by as well. Others intend to study all night, but are made so anxious by the lack of time available, they find they can't concentrate. They move directly from procrastination to panic. All they can think is, "I'll never be able to learn it now. It's too late. I'm not going to be able to remember." And as a result, they don't learn and they don't remember.

WHY WE PROCRASTINATE

We all have the same reasons for procrastinating.

We don't want to do what needs to be done. Some people use procrastination as an avoidance strategy. For example, a man might promise to wash the car—but then deliberately "not get around to it" because (a) he hopes it will rain, in which case it would not make sense to wash the car, or (b) he thinks his wife will get tired of waiting, in which case she will wash it for him. Someone else might postpone starting work on a boring report hoping that the boss will forget having asked for it. This sort of procrastination is not a problem if the strategy works. But it can be a problem if the car remains dirty or the boss gets impatient and snarly.

We think the deed to be done is dumb. There is a natural tendency to put off things that we think don't *deserve* doing. The existential philosopher wants to see the meaning or purpose in an assignment . . . wants to understand the relevance of the deed to daily life. Unfortunately, sometimes the only meaning or purpose of a task is to avoid being fired or pass a course or avoid another argument.

We lack confidence in our ability and don't want to supply final proof of inadequacy. The message running through our brain is, "It won't be good enough. It won't be as good as what others are doing. I will be humiliated."

We are offered two choices and . . . . following another natural tendency . . . we opt for the easy over the hard, the pleasurable over the boring, or the instantly gratifying over satisfaction that must be deferred until a goal is reached.

Should we climb up on the roof and clean leaves out of the gutter—or watch TV? Should we scrub the bathroom floor or go shopping? Should husband and wife have the fight they know is coming to settle a difference of opinion about money—or enjoy a day at the beach? Is it hard to figure out why so many people choose the latter rather than the former?

POSTPONEMENT TECHNIQUES

The art of putting things off is fairly well developed. You are probably familiar with many of the techniques.

- You reward yourself before doing what you probably won't get around to doing anyway. Does this sound familiar? "I'll get to it right after I finish this plate of ice cream"—or as soon as this program is over, or right after the party, or after a good night's rest, or after the football game is over, etc.

- You estimate the time and decide not enough of it is available. You say, "There's no point in starting now. I'd have to stop in ten minutes."

- You con yourself into feeling virtuous by doing something else instead of the right thing, like cleaning off the desk when you had intended to fill out your tax return or getting the car washed instead of tackling the bills.

- You escape into fantasy, which provides immediate enjoyment—like dreaming of being a famous writer—but you never sit down to write.

THE WOULDA/COULDA/SHOULDA RESULT

Immediate enjoyment is what procrastination is all about. Ice cream instead of struggle.

You won't consider procrastination a problem unless you know, deep down, a day of reckoning is bound to come someday. You may avoid the task, but you may not be able to avoid at some point in the future the consequences of *not* doing it.

You may end up with problems that land you in woulda/coulda/shoulda land. Those problems will not necessarily be serious. Getting a low grade on one test does not necessarily mean you'll flunk the course. Not doing a job as well as you might have if you'd devoted more time to it doesn't mean you will botch it completely. Still, these are not problems that can be lightly dismissed, either. People will be annoyed at you for letting them down. That can have unpleasant consequences. You may feel you have let yourself down. Even if your self-esteem is not destroyed, it can be chipped.

NOW RATHER THAN THEN

As with any woulda/coulda/shoulda dilemma, the remedy lies in formulating thought patterns that lead to action. There really is a "doer" mind-set, just as there is a put-it-off mind-set. If you want to be a doer, you must:

Reward yourself for work accomplished rather than for work promised. That is, instead of saying, "I'll do it as soon as I finish this more enjoyable pursuit," you have to say, "I'll permit myself to enjoy a more enjoyable pursuit, but only *after* I get this dog of a job done."

Recognize the excuse for what it is and refuse to accept it. That is, instead of saying, "I don't have enough time to do the whole thing," you must say, "If I can spend ten minutes on it now, I'll have less to do later. You know when cleaning the desk is necessary and when you are diverting yourself from the task at hand.

Set aside a definite time for doing whatever it is you have to do. If you hear yourself say, "As soon as I can fit it in," you know you are in trouble.

Set a deadline for yourself. This can be difficult to arrange, since by definition any self-set deadline is arbitrary and "unofficial." Still, making a deadline puts you in control of yourself—and most people feel better when they are "in charge."

Sometimes the problem is only that you are not confident that you *can* meet a deadline. For example, would you be willing to hand a friend five thousand dollars with instructions to return it to you with interest if you meet your dead-

line, but to donate it to a cause you despise should you fail?
Most people would say no to that question, because they
don't want to risk the possibility of losing five thousand dollars. They think they just might lose it because they aren't
confident of their own ability to do whatever is the task at
hand. And yet, in most cases, when five thousand dollars
really is at stake, people do make their deadline and even
finish before it.

*Confront what you are thinking when your thoughts turn to put-
ting it off.* When you say, "I don't feel like doing it right
now," are you really saying, "I'm afraid to do it, it won't be
perfect"? Once you recognize that thought, you can challenge
it. You can ask yourself, "Is it really so terrible if it's not
perfect? Even if it's only average, isn't something better than
nothing?"

If what you are thinking is, "I hate this project," you can
tell yourself, "Right, but it won't kill me, and the sooner I
get it done, the sooner I can do something else." When you
hear yourself say, "I'll do it right after . . ." you can catch
yourself and say, "There I go again. . . . Better do it now."
When you hear yourself say, "It's too difficult," you can say,
"Do it anyway."

WOULDA/COULDA/SHOULDA BUILDUP

Woulda/coulda/shoulda thinking is a component of everyday
stress and strain: the angst that builds up when you think
you are going to make a mistake that you could have avoided;
the anxiety that builds up when you sense that, in one way or
the other, you are heading for trouble.

These feelings are dismaying enough in and of themselves,
but they carry with them a greater danger—the danger of a
woulda/coulda/shoulda buildup.

What often happens in these minor situations is that we begin to view them in a major way. You start out by making a silly mistake—like forgetting about the bridge construction and ending in a traffic jam—and you berate yourself for that. Then, weeks or maybe even months later, some other minor frustration occurs. Your mind then connects that previous frustration to this new one. You then say, "I can't believe I did this again." Or you might think, "I must really be stupid to allow this to happen again."

Then, something else happens—another minor mistake—but the brain acts as a magnet to pull that one toward the two previous ones in your thoughts. Now, you believe that a pattern is emerging—a pattern that you distort through selective editing (you see only the mistakes you have made recently, while forgetting everything you have done right) and minimizing (even if you can remember some things you have done right, you put *greater importance* on the mistakes).

The result is that you think this clump of minor mistakes is a major problem. This is precisely how generalized feelings of "losing it," of "never doing anything right," of "missing out somewhere," get started—and grow. You can avoid this by recognizing woulda/coulda/shoulda thinking even when the consequences are small.

For example, you forget to mail an important letter—you get home and it's still in your pocket. You think, "Oh no . . . what a goof-up." A week later, you leave the office without a report you had intended to work on at home. You think, "Oh no, what a goof-up *I am!*" A month later, you go to the parking lot to pick up your car, and remember—only after vainly looking for it—that today you parked in the street, next to a meter. And you think, "My mind is going. This is the proof of it. I can't remember *anything* anymore. I can't do anything right."

You can feel yourself becoming distraught. You are poised

for a dive into a woulda/coulda/shoulda whirlpool in which thoughts of having done "everything wrong" swirl around you. It is at this point that you must say, "STOP! What is the evidence that what I claim is true? Am I really a bad, stupid person? What exactly have I done wrong lately?

—Forgot to mail a letter.
—Forgot to bring the report home.
—Forgot where I parked my car.
—All within a period of one month.

In that same month, have I also remembered to mail letters, to bring reports home, to recall where my car was parked, and to accomplish other tasks as well?

The answer is likely to be yes. If you analyze what you were thinking, you will realize that you were selectively editing or minimizing—omitting or downgrading evidence of successful past performance. You were also catastrophizing—jumping to the conclusion that three minor mistakes in three months equals loss of sanity, loss of ability, the end of your world. You were assuming that three mistakes "prove" you are stupid, unworthy, hopeless. When you bring your common sense to bear on the subject, you will realize that "everybody makes mistakes." That may be generalizing—but it is generalizing in a positive, rather than a negative, direction.

CULTURAL PRESSURES

It's almost impossible to be completely free of "everyday" woulda/coulda/shoulda thinking in twentieth-century America—it goes with the territory, you might say.

That can't be said about long-term woulda/coulda/shoulda thinking. After all, it would be hard to argue that the unhappiness someone might feel about taking the "wrong" path in life today is any different from the unhappiness Napoleon felt after Waterloo ("If only I'd realized what the duke of Wellington was up to").

But to some extent our culture imposes a degree of pressure on us that leads to a woulda/coulda/shoulda mind-set. In some areas of the country, for example, people feel it is a crime to waste time. Therefore, they are much more likely to go through the agony of woulda/coulda/shoulda recrimination when stuck in traffic. Some people get upset when they get stuck in traffic even if they aren't going anywhere in particular and therefore can't actually claim to be "late."

Many of us are cursed by the American cultural desire for instant solutions. Some people even start feeling stressed if they have to wait in line at a fast-food counter. They feel entitled to be served immediately—and will get angry if that is not the case. To these people, a "leisurely meal" is when you sit down at McDonald's instead of "ordering to go." There was a time when it took three seconds for a picture to appear after a television set was turned on. Then the "instant on" was invented, and TV sales zoomed. People didn't want to wait *three seconds*!

This cultural trait becomes a woulda/coulda/shoulda problem when you impose an unrealistic standard of "instant solution" upon yourself. It is a good idea to set a deadline, because that may prevent you from procrastinating your way into inaction—but it is *not* a good idea to set *impossible* deadlines. And that is something many of us do.

"I'll finish work early, so that I can take Susie to get her hair cut, stop at the supermarket to shop, pick up the shoes at the repair shop, make dinner, pick up the sitter, and leave in time to talk to Martha before the Civic Association meeting starts. . . ."

"Oh dear, I'm not going to finish in time. Susie may miss

her haircut. What will I have for dinner? I need those shoes. Martha will be furious. . . . I'm so disorganized. I should be able to handle it, but I can't. I don't know what everybody expects of me. . . ."

Hold it. Who is *everybody?* Exactly *what* does everybody expect? Was it not *you* who set this particular set of deadlines? Are those deadlines *realistic?* Have you been *fair* to yourself? Does it make *sense* to assign yourself a schedule that requires the timing of a precision flying team? Isn't it possible that, as the TV commercial puts it, you deserve a break today?

Chapter Thirteen

"THEM"—RESISTING PRESSURE FROM OTHERS

"If you'd listened to me . . ."
"You should never have done that. . . ."
"What a shame you didn't think of it earlier. . . ."
"If only you had stopped before it was too late . . ."
"You could have made something of yourself, but . . ."
"If only you had taken Michael with you that day . . ."
"Why didn't we leave when we had the chance?"

These are the lyrics of the woulda/coulda/shoulda chorus. These are the words of all those "helpful" people who are only too willing to step forward and let you know where you went wrong, how right *they* were, how all your problems—and possibly their problems, too—could have been avoided, if only . . .

It seems so unfair. You are determined to make a fresh start and move ahead in your life—but "they" won't let you. You now realize that endlessly debating what you could or should have done in the past doesn't help anybody. But "they" insist on continuing the debate. You know that moving ahead means planning what you will do next. But "they" insist on reviewing over and over and over again what you did before. What can you do about "them"?

Who are "they?" Anyone who is not you. Family, friends, co-workers, neighbors, strangers, society, the world. Anybody who reminds you—and reminds you and reminds you—of your past missteps, mistakes, and omissions.

Maybe they are not very specific about it. They simply let you know they think you made a wrong turn somewhere. They may berate you for not measuring up. Or maybe they zero in on one particular wrong or bungle.

—"If you'd taken that job Joe offered you, you would be a partner by now."
—"If you'd bought the stock when it was selling at eighteen, we'd be rich."
—"If we'd saved more when we were young, we wouldn't have to sell the house now. Why didn't you save money? You spent and spent and spent, and now look at us. . . ."
—"If you had been nicer to Ben, you two would still be together. . . ."

They may even dwell on the fact that you have been unlucky! Burn victims, for example, tell of family members who seem unable to stop saying, "If only you hadn't taken that plane, if only you were not in that car, if only you had gone to Los Angeles that day" . . . . as if saying "if only" could retroactively put out the fire.

If you have one or more of "them" in your life, you know how emotionally draining it can be to be constantly reminded of something you already feel terrible about. It wears away your spirit in the same way drops of water wear away stone. You probably have tried to stop them. You argue. You point out that they don't have all the facts right. You grovel. "Will you please drop it?" you yell. You explain. You discuss what you might have done differently for the ninety-millionth time. But soon they are back again, tormenting you anew with the same woulda/coulda/shoulda litany. Is the only answer to move away so that you neither see nor hear from "them" again?

No. That might not even be possible. But, luckily, there

are other ways to cope with woulda/coulda/shoulda from others.

BASIC WOULDA/COULDA/SHOULDA DEFENSE

The next time "they" come after you . . . the next time one of "them" brings up the subject of what would or could or should have happened in your past, refuse to argue. Refuse the opportunity to debate.

The situation you face is this: You cannot control what "they" say. But you can control what *you* say. If someone tries to engage you in a verbal tug-of-war that you know you can't win, you can always refuse to play.

You know that in a real tug-of-war—the kind where competitors tug on either end of a rope in hopes of pulling the opposition over to their side, there is no game if the rope is pulled on only one side. When "they" give you a woulda/coulda/shoulda lecture, they are holding one end of the rope and trying to goad you into picking up the other end. We're tempted to advise, "Just say no," but there is a bit more to it than that.

DISARMING TECHNIQUE

The simplest method of not getting involved in a verbal tug-of-war is known in psychological terms as a "disarming technique." Admittedly, this technique will not work with hard-core woulda/coulda/shoulda thinkers. But it may be sufficient in some cases. Disarming technique involves admitting you are wrong before the other side gets a chance to accuse you.

Suppose, for example, that you perform poorly on some project at work. You slink into the office the next day, hoping nobody notices you. Unfortunately, that doesn't work. When confronted, you get defensive; you make excuses; you blame others. But the boss doesn't buy any of it. The boss yells, screams, threatens. The boss drags up other examples of poor performance. One word leads to another. You can see that no good is going to come out of this.

But suppose that instead of trying to avoid blame, you openly invite it. You walk into the boss's office and say, "I'd like to apologize for that report I turned in. It's not my best work and I know it. I'd like a chance to redo it." The boss may still be furious . . . but by confessing, apologizing, and requesting mercy before you are accused, you take the angry words the boss has been mentally rehearsing right out of his or her mouth. As often as not, this has a very calming effect.

The boss has to think of something else to say. Maybe it will be, "Yes, do it again and do it right this time." Or, "Never mind, this is good enough for now, but do better in the future." Or, "It's too late now, but at least you see the error of your ways." But whatever the boss says is likely to be shorter—and quieter!—than it would have been otherwise.

Disarming technique can work in many situations. Imagine yourself about to approach a gate agent at the airport with a request to change your seat assignment. You can see that this agent is overworked and harassed and probably just in the mood to snarl at you, "Sorry, but it's too late and there's nothing I can do."

What do you do? You admit that you are the nuisance you know yourself to be. You say, "I hate to bother you when I can see you already have too much to do, but it would be a big help to me if you could change my seat assignment. If you can't, I'll understand. But I would really appreciate anything you can do." As often as not, that busy agent will help you, if it is at all possible to do so.

Why does disarming technique work so well? Because most people are—and want to be—decent, helpful human beings. That's why. That's not true of everybody, of course. Some people truly enjoy being nasty, and will be nasty no matter what you say or do. Some people are so absorbed in their own unhappiness, they aren't capable of being helpful. But most people will react with generosity to someone who admits being in the wrong.

How do you use this technique with someone who insists on giving you an unwanted woulda/coulda/shoulda lecture?

You simply say, "You're right. I agree."

You don't try to defend yourself. You don't point out that your accuser doesn't have the facts straight. You don't accuse the person of nagging or harassing you. You agree.

But what if the haranguer is *not* right? you ask. What if he or she *has* twisted the facts? What if you are not entirely to blame? What if the haranguer has done even worse? What if . . .

It doesn't matter. Your object here is not to straighten out the historical record. Your object here is to get this woulda/coulda/shoulda haranguer off your case. And the way to do that is to agree and be done with it.

The haranguer may say, "Of course I'm right. That's what I've been telling you. You should have done what you could have done, and if you had done that, then you would (or we would or everybody would) be better off today. . . ."

And your response is, "I don't want to argue about it. You're right, but it's in the past and I feel that arguing about the past is not productive. I'd rather talk about what I (or we) should do next."

That puts the burden on the holder of the rope to come up with something else to say. And some people will see your point and drop their end of the rope.

THE TOUGH-IT-OUT RESPONSE

But not everybody. If "they" have been nagging at you with a woulda/coulda/shoulda theme for years, no simple admission of wrong on your part will even slow them down, much less stop them cold. Combatting the long-term and determined woulda/coulda/shoulda lecturer requires greater effort. But the basic strategy remains the same—refusing to pick up the other end of the tug-of-war rope.

Obviously, you would like "them" to simply shut up. But telling them that hasn't gotten you anywhere. Telling them that a hundred times hasn't gotten you anywhere.

You say, "Fine, whatever you say."

"They" say, "That's not an answer."

You say, "You are right."

"They" say, "Of course I'm right. That's what I've been telling you."

You say, "I agree with you."

"They" say, "You're just saying that. You don't really think it, even though it's true. If you don't mean it, don't say it."

You say, "You are right."

"They" say, "If I'm right, then why didn't you listen to me then?"

And on and on and on.

What now?

Now, you must forget about trying to get "them" to stop talking and concentrate harder on getting yourself to *stop listening*. Concentrate on giving less weight to what "they" say. *Concentrate on not picking up the rope.*

You know that nothing is to be gained by going over the same ground again and again. So you must tell "them" that you feel nothing is to be gained by going over the same ground again and again—and you will not do it. You may say, "This is destructive to our relationship. I don't want to argue about this again and I won't. You may keep talking, but I will not listen. If I must leave the room, I will leave it. But I will not pick up the rope."

After you have made this point, you don't have to go into elaborate explanations every time "they" bring up the subject. You merely say, *"Sorry, but that subject is off-limits. That subject is a no-no. I can't talk about that." You might just say, "I think it would be a good idea for me to go watch TV now," or "I'm going to take a walk."

THE INEVITABLE ESCALATION

What will happen next—and you can count on it—is an escalation of "their" effort to get you into this tug-of-war.

"Please talk to me about this. Please pick up your end of the rope."

"No."

"Only a coward would refuse to discuss this. You are afraid to pick up the rope."

"Not interested."

"You don't listen to me. You never listen to me."

"I'll listen to you talk about another subject."

"You are a yellow-bellied, spineless, dirty polecat skunk if you don't pick up the rope."

(Silence.)

"Your friends would discuss this like grown-ups." (Silence.) "Your brother would pick up the rope." (Silence.) "Your father, may he rest in peace, would pick up the rope." (Silence.) "If you loved me, you would pick up the rope." (Silence.) "You don't care about me. If you cared about me, you'd respond when I talk to you." (Silence.)

Don't pick up the rope. No matter what. Because once you get involved in a woulda/coulda/shoulda argument, you will not only stir up every negative feeling associated with the past, you will also—and this almost invariably happens—find yourself involved in all kinds of peripheral, and equally useless, fights.

You are likely to find yourself arguing not only about what you should have done, but about what others should have done or what others thought at the time. For example: "Your former teammate could have helped, but he didn't." Now, you find yourself defending your old teammate, even though you don't know whether he could have helped or whether it would have made any difference if he had. You haven't seen your teammate in years. You haven't even thought about him. And here you are getting into a tussle on his behalf!

ROPE GAMESMANSHIP

Expecting this escalation to come prepares you to deal with it. There is no better armament you can wear than awareness. Being alert to the opposition's strategy can enable you to achieve a certain distance. You might even develop an interest in hearing the escalation take place. "What will "they" say next to get me to pick up the rope? Oh my, that was a clever gambit. But that won't fool me, either. I'm not playing."

Threats, insults, tears, screaming. All expected. All ignored.

THE EXTINCTION PHENOMENON

What may then happen—even if not anywhere near as soon as you would like—is that the woulda/coulda/shoulda lectures will slow to a trickle or even cease.

This is due to the extinction phenomenon. Psychological research has found that behavior that is not reinforced tends to stop. When a particular behavior gets no response over a period of time, the behavior becomes extinct. When "they" find that they never get a rise out of you with their woulda/coulda/shoulda accusations, they just might give up. The accusations eventually disappear. It's just no fun playing tug-of-war alone.

When this extinction phenomenon occurs, you will probably feel a temptation to let down your guard. Be warned that this can be very dangerous.

The first danger you face is called spontaneous recovery. Here's what happens. The fire seems to be out. "They" have not brought up the woulda/coulda/shoulda lecture for two years now. But then, out of nowhere, or maybe out of a bad mood, "they" bring it up again.

You may think, "Well, after all this time, I guess I can discuss it."

No, you can't. If you start to argue, you will find the debate will once again rage at its *previous highest level*. Just one slip, and you will have to start the whole extinction process over again. This is one of those truisms of human nature that therapists hear about over and over and over again.

Don't even reply, "Why do you bring this up again after all this time? I thought we had an understanding." That alone is like opening the door and allowing the hurricane to blow through the house. Stick to the tried and true: "I'm sorry. I just don't want to talk about that. It's not productive."

The second dangerous area, once some time has gone by, is a very natural desire on your part to have "them" understand your point of view. Deep down, you'd like to straighten "them" out about facts of the past that they have wrong, or you'd like "them" to agree with you that it is better to focus on the future. And so, after a reassuring period of calm, *you bring the subject up!* And lo, you find yourself right back where you were before. Don't pick up the rope. Not immediately, and not later, either.

GOING "FISHING"

There's another metaphor that fits the situation we have described just as aptly—and that is "catching a fish on a hook." When you go fishing, you bait the hook and drop it into the water in the well-tested belief that some unsuspecting fish will come along, try to swallow the bait, and end up getting hooked.

But what if the fish thinks your bait looks a little fishy? "It looks tasty enough," says the fish, "but I think there could be a hook hidden in there somewhere." The fish swims off to look for lunch elsewhere.

When others try to entice you into another woulda/coulda/shoulda debate, they are, in effect, baiting a hook and waiting for you to swallow it. It may be very tempting bait.

The better you know this woulda/coulda/shoulda person in your life, the more enticing their bait is likely to be. After all, the people we know best know best how to push our buttons. They know exactly what will successfully lure us. If you want to catch a flounder, you use minnows—not a hundred-dollar bill, because fish don't care about money. If you want to catch lake trout, a feathered fly is better.

Usually, "they" will bait you with whatever has worked before. Therefore, it is up to you to make sure it doesn't work again. You want to fight. You want to straighten them out. You want to catalog *their* faults for them in return. You want to scream about how sick you are of hearing what they have to say. But once you do that, you have taken the bait— and you are on the hook. Once you do that, "they" can reel you in, once again, to continuing woulda/coulda/shoulda speculation that will not help you move forward in your life.

"Why didn't you listen to me? If you had bought that

property we were offered, we would be as well off as the Joneses."

A delicious morsel is dangling before your eyes.

Maybe you could just nibble at the edges:

"You never told me to buy it." "You know we didn't have the money to buy it." "The Joneses are well off for reasons other than buying property." "The indications at the time were that it was a poor investment." "I was busy with other things and I didn't have the time to look into it." "And how about that opportunity you had, which you totally ignored?"

Remember, however, that if you nibble, you risk becoming hooked. And that means you find yourself continuing a conflict that has no end because it has no answer. You cannot rewrite the past. You can only feel bad about it. So once again you feel bad, you feel guilty, you reinforce your loss. If you merely say, "Why don't you leave it alone?" . . . you've been hooked.

THE GUILT RESPONSE

You may feel obliged to be reeled in—to pick up the end of the tug-of-war rope—because you feel guilty. It could be that when you say "they" are right, you know that to be completely true.

"They" said, "Don't drive so fast." But you did and got into an accident. "They" said, "Don't invest in that stock, it's a loser." But you thought you knew better—and you were wrong. "They" said, "Don't rush into this marriage." But you said, "Stop trying to run my life. I know what I'm doing." So you can't blame "them" for saying, "I told you so."

But let us repeat again, *It does not matter whether what "they" say is accurate or not.* If you agree to argue about the past in any way, you are on the hook. And if you are on the hook, you are doomed to dangle and struggle and feel miserable. Debating the past will not change the past. Debating the past will not change the present or the future.

WHY DO "THEY" WANT TO TALK ABOUT THE PAST?

Maybe you have asked yourself, "Why do 'they' keep bringing this up? Can't 'they' see how unhappy they are making me?"

It's not that "they" are mean, vicious, heartless, and unfeeling. There are all kinds of reasons why otherwise reasonable people feel a need to impose their woulda/coulda/shoulda comments on others.

Some people just can't help being woulda/coulda/shoulda thinkers. They learned this mode of thought from childhood, and, like it or not, they are, in the words of an old song, "just doin' what comes naturally."

For some, it's sport. Really. Getting somebody upset, angry, guilty, can indeed be just like having a huge fish battling on the other end of the line. It's exciting. It's a power trip.

For some, it's a defensive measure. Examining *your* errors postpones an examination of *theirs,* either by you or by their own consciences. It may be that rather than take responsibility for themselves, it's simply easier to shift the blame— as in, "If only you had done this or that, I'd be happy today."

Some people actually enjoy the feeling of martyrdom that comes from either having been—or merely perceiving themselves as having been—victimized by another. To bring up the wrong that was done over and over reinforces that delightful feeling of "poor little me."

Some people really like being "right" and want to relive that special feeling as often as possible, even if it's at your expense. "If you had listened to superior, incredible, wonderful, infallible me, the world would be a better place today. Pardon me while I pat myself on the back again."

Some people do it because they feel guilty about being in the wrong themselves. They feel that if they apologize over and over and cry about it over and over, this somehow expunges their guilt. A grandmother who cries every time she sees the scars on her grandchild that were caused by her careless driving doesn't comprehend that this behavior makes the child even more uncomfortable.

Some may truly feel that when they review the past, they are doing so "for your own good"—the way parents of small children say, "If you had listened to me, you wouldn't have burned your hand on the hot stove." No one would deny that a lecture on what we should have done, immediately after we have done the wrong thing, can be a very effective learning technique.

Thus, most of us get a good solid helping of "if you'd listened to me, then you wouldn't be in this mess" as we are growing up. It's a system many parents use to pass along what they have learned to the next generation. "Didn't I tell you that if you leave the door open, the dog will get out? You left the door open and the dog got out. See what happens when you don't listen to me?" Some parents reinforce the message by calling upon powerful allies. As in, "You didn't do what I told you to do and you got hurt. Serves you right. God is punishing you for not listening to me."

Unfortunately, some parents and others don't know when to stop. They cannot recognize when, through too much repetition, that helpful learning technique turns into an obstacle to progress—when too much focusing on what was done wrong inhibits the ability to do the next thing right—or to do any next thing at all.

Matt's parents felt they were being helpful by pointing out his failings. They felt it would help him improve. If he showed them a painting, they said, "Don't you think the sky is a little too blue?" If he showed them a test on which he'd received a "B," they said, "You shouldn't have missed those two questions. They were easy ones." Matt became discouraged. "What's the point of trying?" he said. "I'm always going to be a failure."

In some cases, incessant woulda/coulda/shoulda tug-of-wars are a symptom of an unhealthy family system. There is a psychological theory that holds that all systems—even family systems—are most comfortable operating in a state of balance. If one side tilts the balance, the other side will move to restore the old balance. Thus, if you come from a family of woulda/coulda/shoulda thinkers and you decide to break away and focus on what you can do next to improve your present and future, you are likely to find that this puts the rest of the family off balance. And without even realizing what they are doing, they move to pull you back into the accustomed pattern.

YES, BUT . . .

There are two ways that woulda/coulda/shoulda others try to pull us back into the pattern of the past—to keep us on the hook. The first is the repeated woulda/coulda/shoulda nagging that we have described. The second, just as destructive, is to *interrupt whatever effort you may make to try to break out of the past.*

Whenever you come up with a Plan A or Plan B that will move you forward in your life, "They" will say, "Yes, but . . ."

—"*Yes,* you may be able to go back to school, *but* think how old you will be when you graduate."

—"*Yes,* you could quit your job, *but* you probably can't get another as good at this stage of your life."

—"*Yes,* I agree you should stop moping around and do something, *but . . .*"

The woulda/coulda/shoulda person says, "If you had listened to me, you could have been a doctor." You say, "You're right, but I have decided to become a nurse. I have learned that I can take courses at night and acquire a nursing degree in three years." The woulda/coulda/shoulda person says, "But being a doctor would have been better," or "You're too old to go to nursing school," or "That's no job for a man," or "If you had gone to nursing school years ago, you'd be the head nurse today." You can feel your enthusiasm evaporating.

Whenever you say, "I want to look forward now," "they" come up with a reason to keep you looking back over your shoulder. You want that other person to say, "Great idea. I'm pleased for you. I will support you." But it doesn't happen.

Let's face it. All of the errors of thinking that we have discussed in this book are human errors that anyone can make and that most people make at one time or another. That means that just as it is possible for *you* to jump to wrong conclusions and thus talk yourself out of taking some action that might improve your lot, it's equally possible for *someone else* to do exactly the same thing.

Maybe "they" are perfectionists who, in their own lives, can't see the point of making a move unless it will accomplish everything they desire, not merely move closer to that accomplishment, not merely achieve a piece of it. And so, "they" don't see any point in *you* making a move if that move is not "perfect."

Maybe "they" believe they can foretell the future—even if

no one else can. Therefore, they "helpfully" foretell it for you by saying it won't work, it can't happen. "Take it from me, there is no point in trying," they say. "Don't even waste your time."

In short, "they" may be quite honestly telling you how they see things. But, honest or not, they aren't much help, because they are looking backward and thus can't really see what's ahead. That is definitely not the best kind of guide to have.

CHANGING "THEM"

"Is there *nothing* I can do to change 'them,'" you ask?

You are hardly unusual if you want "them"—whoever "they" are in your life—to understand and support your need to move forward. You may be saying, "I realize I may be able to stop the woulda/coulda/shoulda lectures by not responding to them and that I may be able to stop the 'yes, but' attacks by not revealing any of my plans, but. . . . I'd really much rather change 'them.'"

You can try. You probably will try. And you may even succeed. Maybe, in your situation, it's possible to reach "them" and make "them" aware of how the things they say hurt your feelings and make you angry and unhappy. You can relate what you have learned in this book. You might hand "them" the book and suggest reading certain passages you have marked.

You have the most chance of succeeding if you try to have your conversation with the woulda/coulda/shoulda person in your life at the "right" time—that is, at a time when you have the other person's undivided attention. You cannot get someone's undivided attention if one child is crying and another has taken all the pots out of the kitchen closet. You cannot get someone's undivided attention when the telephone is ringing, when the Super Bowl is on TV, when it is eleven o'clock at night and the person is dead tired.

You will have the best chance of getting your message across if you prepare what you plan to say in advance. The idea of preparing a script for a conversation with someone you know very well may strike you as strange. Shouldn't a conversation be spontaneous? Spontaneity is nice, but when you want what you say to count, it's better to be prepared. Johnny Carson and David Letterman are not spontaneous— though they may sound that way. Both have writers who think up clever lines for them to say. Most successful public speakers are not spontaneous. At the very least, they have thought through what they plan to talk about, and have written "cue" cards to remind them of the pertinent points, even if they haven't written out every word.

When dealing with "them," it helps to have thought through what you want to say in advance—particularly since you already have a good idea of what "they" will say, having heard it several times already.

When you prepare your personal script, be positive. Negative comments, even if justified, only stir up more recriminations.

Thus: "I know that you want to help me, and I need to talk to you about our conversations."

Not: "You are always bugging me."

Not: "I'm sick and tired of your nagging."

Not: "If you continue nagging me, I'm going to punch out your lights."

Think about the points you want to make. Write them down. Try the script out on a friend. Practice it.

You might say, "I want to talk to you about what I/we can do today or tomorrow. It's understandable to be upset about the past, but I want to talk about what I/we are going to do now to improve the future. I want to talk to you about the options I/we have now. If you think it's worth it to keep going over the past, by all means continue. That's up to you. I am only saying that I will not pick up the rope."

You might say, "You know what would be helpful for me—if you would be supportive in what I am doing now. Let's talk about what we can do together to move forward. I believe we can do more together than I can do alone. But if I must do it alone, I will."

You might say, "Do you have a suggestion to make about what I/we should do next? What is your suggestion?"

Sometimes the woulda/coulda/shoulda debate is not the real issue. The person is angry and looks for something to fight about that is different from whatever is really bothering him or her. This is always dangerous, because the real issue doesn't get resolved and continues to grow. You might ask, "Is this the real problem? Is there something else bothering you that we should talk about?"

Sometimes persuading the other person to agree to move forward is not the same as persuading the other person to adopt *your* plan for moving forward. Suppose the situation were this: A bad investment has caused you serious financial losses. You finally persuade your spouse that it is useless to continue to bemoan the unwise decision—you must discuss what you will do next. Now it turns out that you think you should sell the house and move to a less expensive neighborhood, but your spouse says, "Never." This is not a perfect world, and you may not always agree. But you can agree to collect data, to get as much information as possible to lead to a mutually satisfying decision. There is hope in arguing over a plan. There is only hopelessness in arguing over the past.

TRY, TRY AGAIN . . . AND THEN QUIT

But what if your effort to get "their" agreement and support doesn't go well at all? What if, after you have explained the uselessness of talking about the past, they bring up the past again? You can try again to reach them.

But set yourself a five-session limit!

Once you realize that you have had the exact same discussion five times and the other person is insistent upon returning to woulda/coulda/shoulda and "yes, but"—it's time to quit. There are certain situations in which trying again works, and other situations in which trying something else works better. If trying to change "them" doesn't work after you have made five efforts, you will have to seek elsewhere for advice and support.

If you say, "Maybe I'll try to reach them one more time, maybe seven is the magic number, maybe eight attempts will do it . . ." you are still on the hook. You know when your message is not getting through. You know that when you have been having the exact same debate for the last twelve months—or the last twelve years—"they" are not going to change their views. People change only when they want to, and if the people you are dealing with don't want to change, they won't. The only sensible way to deal with that is simply to allow them to keep their views while acting on your own. And as we said before, you do that by refusing to be drawn into a woulda/coulda/shoulda debate.

Does that mean surrendering to "their" point of view? No, it means not taking the hook. It means rejecting the bait and remaining a free fish. Remember, all that it takes for the fish to escape is to keep its big mouth shut.

But, you argue, I don't want to give "them" the satisfaction of thinking they are right when they are not. No, you don't want to give "them" that satisfaction, but what price are you willing to pay to deny them that satisfaction? Remember what we said in the chapter about revenge. You may not *want* to let someone get away with injustice, but if the only way to "get them" is to sacrifice yourself in the process, consider carefully how badly you want to "get them."

You may think, "I just want to make one little point and then I'll let it go." The fish says, "I won't try to eat all of the bait—I'm too smart for that—but I'll just nibble this corner here." And ends up stuck on a prong. The fish may get away—but only after an exhausting battle, only after suffering a wounded jaw. Was the little bite of bait worth it?

You may say, "I don't disagree at all with "their" assessment of what went wrong; all I want to argue about is the effect it has had. They claim that the fact that I didn't take that job offer has stunted my career. I agree that I should have taken the job offer. I only want them to admit it wasn't as good an offer as they think . . . that I wouldn't have done *that much* better."

You are wasting your time, because you are arguing about what might have been—and that is something no one knows. "They" don't know, and you don't either. You may find "their" viewpoint annoying, but is it really worth fighting about?

Let us say you are walking down the street. A stranger stares right at you and says, "How amazing to see a kangaroo hopping down Main Street!"

—Do you immediately thump your tail on the ground and start hopping?
—Do you run after this stranger and say, "You are mistaken, sir, I am not a kangaroo. Kangaroos are marsupials, which are found only in zoos and Australia. I, however, am a human being. . . ."
—Do you worry about not giving the speaker the "satisfaction" of thinking that you are a kangaroo?

Or do you merely shrug your shoulders, say, "Poor guy can't tell a human from a kangaroo,"—and *go on about your business?*

How much time would you spend defending yourself against the charge that you are a kangaroo? How much time do you want to spend defending yourself against what might have been had you done something differently—when you can't go back and change what you have done? Better to go on about your business. Better to go on to do whatever it is that you can do *now*.

"They" may continue to try to bait you. Just remember that "they" will give up the effort much more quickly once they realize they aren't having the same effect.

JOINING "THEM"

If "they" have ever given you trouble, you may find it hard to believe that you could ever become one of "them." But it happens. It happens because "themhood" is something that grows over the years. It happens because we are not always aware that we are giving "helpful advice" in a woulda/coulda/shoulda way.

You see someone close to you—child, spouse, colleague—do something that you believe he or she could have and should have avoided. And you say, "You should have been more careful." Or, "This wouldn't have happened if you had listened to me."

You may say that you are only telling the person what he or she should know for his or her own good, that the person would be better off if he or she listened to your wise counsel. That may be true.

But the question you must ask yourself is, "What are the results of my admonitions?" When you remind others of their lapses, does it galvanize them to action or ensure that nothing will happen? Does your commentary help them or merely engender resentment against you? Do you enjoy being resented?

You do not have to ignore the situation. But you also do not need to wave a finger under another's nose to get your point across. You need only *not* phrase your commentary in a woulda/coulda/shoulda manner. That is, you might say, "Yes, it would have been better if you had studied, but that is past now. What do you plan to do next?"

DEALING WITH UNTOUCHABLES

One final note: There is a certain group of "them" who are unreachable because they are untouchable because they do not physically exist. If this situation were a science-fiction movie, it would be called *They Come from Inner Space,* because the problem here is not so much what "they" think, as what *we* think "they" think.

One can continue to be pressured by someone who has been dead for twenty years. We are influenced by perceived criticism of departed parents, departed spouses, people we used to know and have lost touch with. We know what "they" would say if they were here. We hear what "they" say. "They" are telling us we should have or could have done better, done more, done it differently. We feel deeply that we have let "them" down, and that feeling is a persistent presence.

How does one deal with that?

The same way you deal with any of "them." You concede "they" were right. And go on about your business. You may concede that "they" were disappointed. And go on about your life.

We may never be able to change the way "they" see things. We can only change the way *we* see things. We can only change what we do.

Your future is not up to "them." It's up to you.

Chapter Fourteen

WILL/CAN/SHALL

Banishing woulda/coulda/shoulda thinking from your life does not mean you will never again look back. Even if you wanted to permanently erase the past, it would be impossible to do. People simply don't *decide* to have amnesia.

But the message of this book is that it is possible to learn to look back in *a new way*.

THE HALL OF MEMORIES

Somewhere inside all of us there is a Hall of Memories where we keep the people, places, and events of our past. A trip to this Hall of Memories can be triggered by a word, a sight, a smell, or a taste. If you bite into a cookie just like those your mother baked, it may well evoke a flood of memories about Mom. If you hear the song that was popular when you were in high school, you may feel a wave of nostalgia flow over you.

These memories may be bittersweet . . . like a middle-aged man recalling his days as a teenage football hero. He enjoys remembering the fun he used to have, even if it does unkindly remind him that he'd have a hard time jogging the length of a football field today.

These memories may be instructive. If you confront a situation similar to one you experienced in the past, you may consider handling it differently this time.

These memories may be painful, but only temporarily so, because a trip to the Hall of Memories is like a trip to a museum that you visit both for enjoyment and for education. You inspect the good times here and a disastrous decision there. You might pause for a memorial tribute to a loved one who has died or moved away. But then you return to the present—to your current interests. You come away refreshed, warmed, or warned—ready to deal again with the future. Maybe even able to warn others not to repeat your mistakes.

The key to progress in life is returning to the present. The Hall of Memories becomes a fascinating place to visit—no longer a place in which to live—or even linger.

THE JANUS OUTLOOK

We need to see the past as well as look toward the future. But we need to do this in a balanced way. We call this balance the Janus Outlook—named for Janus, the Roman god of doorways.

Janus is always pictured as having eyes, nose, and mouth on both the front and back of his head. That is so because a doorway is simultaneously both an entrance and exit. When Janus stands in the doorway—the present—he looks forward and backward at the same time. The month of January is named for Janus because it marks the end of the old year, the beginning of the new. Janus learns from where he has been— while keeping two of his eyes focused firmly on where he is going.

Janus is a good role model for all of us who have regrets about our past. We may never forget what we cannot erase— but we need not be disabled by it.

Using the techniques of cognitive therapy, you can now challenge exaggerated and distorted memories—and prevent them from holding you in the past. You learn from looking back—and then set your sights on where you are going. You can enter the doorway asking, "What next?"

> Let us not go over the old ground,
> Let us rather prepare for what is to come.
> —Cicero (106–43 B.C.)

INDEX